Pearls from Upanişads

PEARLS FROM UPANIṢADS

DR. R. B. SHARMA

PARTRIDGE
A Penguin Random House Company

ISBN:	Softcover	978-1-4828-5053-6
	eBook	978-1-4828-5054-3

Print information available on the last page.

To order additional copies of this book, contact
Partridge India
000 800 10062 62
orders.india@partridgepublishing.com

www.partridgepublishing.com/india

Contents

Part One

Part Two

Phonetic Transliteration Table

Vowels (Initial and when combined with consonants).

A a	as in Amar or in karma	[as in ago or bassoon]
Ā ā	as in Atma or in Kama	[as in balm or car]
I i	as in Indra and Iswara or in Kim or karoti or Gārgi	[as in impart or tiffin or taxi]
U	as in Upanişad or in Satru	[as in Uranus or uranium]
oo/u	as in upar or in Bhoota	[as in use or utility or tattoo]
E	as in Ekam or in ken or in Kesava	[as in effort or eight or trainee]
Ai	as in Aisvarya or in kailash	[as in effluent or avail]
O	as in Om or in kopa	[as in omnibus or solo]
Au	as in Ausadha or in kaun	[as in authorize or olive or caucus]
n	as in Angar or in Kansa	[as in lung or singe]
ħ/s	as in āpaħ or in tejaħ	[as in ending the words shudder or umbar]
ŗ	as in ŗşi or in Amrita	[as in ream or ring]

Consonants

The standard Devnagri pronunciation should be followed. Exceptions are given below.

ch	as in Nachiketā
chh	as in Chhanda
tĥ	as in nistha
t	as in atma
th	as in pŗthvi
d	as in deva
dh	as in dhoom, dhyāna
ņ	as in prāņa
ph	as in phala
bh	as in bhu or bhoo
Ś ś	as in satru or in kusa
Ş ş	as in in kosa
s	as in sama or in sansara
kşa	as in ksama or in kaksa
tra	as in trās or in putra
Jņa	as in Jńāna or in yajńa

Introduction

The Upaniṣads have inspired people of all ages in a variety of ways. Some contemplated deeply on the Truth propounded in these treatises and made it an abiding guide in their quest for the Ultimate Bliss. They were the sages. Some others gathered the essence of this 'Secret knowledge' as the bees collect honey and passed on this nectar to the deserving seekers. They were the great masters. Yet others engaged themselves in unfolding the subtleties of the texts through extensive commentaries and explanatory works. They were the Vedic scholars. Many more undertook the task of producing translations of the known texts in contemporary languages. They were the torch bearers of Upaniṣadic teachings. In sum, the appeal of the Upaniṣads remained perennial, universal and above all exhilarating.

Generally, it is believed that since the Upaniṣads deal with matters spiritual they are beyond the purpose and reach of the common man and are meant for the other worldly alone. The truth indeed is different. True, the subject of Upaniṣadic inquiry is the Ultimate Reality alone, but the search has all-through been all-encompassing. In the approach towards unravelling the mystery of existence, the planes of the elements *(adhi-bhutas)*, of the divinities *(adhi-daiva)* and of the self *(adhi-ātam)* together were perceived as an inseparable unity and the seers of these scriptures spared no aspect of 'the being' or the 'non-being' unprobed. Virtually, these sages were concerned as much about the 'here' and 'now' as they were about the 'here-after' and 'yonder'[1]. No wonder, all the major philosophical schools in the land of their origin trace their witness within these treatises.

Since the Upaniṣads neither talk of a God or gods they are not theistic in nature. They do refer to certain deities representing the cosmic forces which are strictly regulated by the cosmic law and therefore can neither be propitiated nor turned hostile in any manner. The Upaniṣads are not religious documents either. They lay down no creed or rituals. Their discourse is entirely secular; as the term is understood today. They are spiritual legacies inherited by humankind cutting across all divides because they only talk of the spirit (Ātman) as one without a second.

---

1 Vivekānanda saw the Vedānta of the Upaniṣads not as a life-negating and other-worldly philosophy but a way of every day life, nay a way of life for every individual, every home and every nation. He traced in them a universal religion leading to the God enshrined in every soul and immanent in nature.

Swami Dayānand Saraswati held that the four Vedas, which comprise the Samhitā-mantra, alone are the words of God. They are free from error and an authority unto themselves. Like the sunlight they reveal not only themselves out also other objects of the universe. He postulated that the Brāhmaṇas, i.e. the commentaries on the Samhitās, the six vedāngas, the six upāngas, the four upvedas and a whole host of shākhās were the expositions of the original texts by the great ṛṣis over a period of time. They are not authorities unto themselves. Incase of contradictions, if any, the Vedic injunctions prevail.

The Upanişads form the third and the final part[2] of the Vedas and so also are known as 'Vedānta' or the end part of the Vedas. The expression Vedānta not only locates their placement in the text of the 'Revealed Knowledge' but also signifies its ultimate message and the crowning glory.

The Hindu concept of 'Revelation' is unique. It neither limits itself to a specific agency (human or divine) nor to a specific time frame. The basal postulate of the Vedānta argument is that knowledge (*Prajñā*) being an aspect of the Timeless is free from the bondage of time. It, therefore, is eternal and self-existent. It can either be discovered or attained but not created. Albeit, 'the Reality' reveals Itself from time to time through some God-filled souls who having received It through intuitive experience communicated the same with divine afflatus for the salvation of others.'

In perspective, it is plausible to believe that at some stage these revelations were pieced together by some great masters in a form and sequence suited to instruct the successive generations. By and by institutions of great learning sprang up in deep forests across the land. In these forest schools the young seekers received the subtle knowledge 'sitting close to the masters'. Hence the term 'Upanişad' (Upa-ni-şada) meaning 'sitting near'. Śankarāchārya has defined[3]

---

2 The other two parts of the Vedas are called 'the *mantras'* and the 'Brāhmaṇas'. A Vedic mantra denotes a hymn or an utterance which has been thought out and communicated and which has the power to save one's soul. The Brāhmaṇas contain explanations of the meanings, importance and procedures of offering different prayers and reciting of hymns and scriptural formulae.

3 Bṛhadāraṇykopanişad, the first part, the first Brāhmaṇa, connecting commentary.

Upanişad as that body of knowledge acquisition of which puts an end to the cycle of births and deaths to which an embodied soul is subjected.

In their textual arrangements, Upanişads consist of two parts *viz.* 'the Upadesa' or the instruction with regard to the recommended meditation and 'the vich*ā*ra' or the metaphysical exposition of the recommended meditation. With the passage of time a large number of texts staked claims to be Upanişads, but traditionally only about a dozen of these are accepted as the major or the Vedic Upanişads.

A common feature of the Upanişads is their ability to communicate whereby even the most subtle of thoughts is expressed in a matter of fact way. To achieve this end, a wide range of devices including parables, dialogues debates, discourses, disputations and monologues were employed. The masters always selected an appropriate technique to elucidate an aphorism, to clarify a statement, to un-twine an etymological puzzle or to highlight an analogical postulation. The purpose always was the clarity of thought and vision. All the same, parables and dialogues remained the popular modes of developing ideas towards logical conclusions and of imparting instruction. In all such parables not only human beings but also animals, birds, celestial beings, elements of nature, gods and even the First Born (Brahm*ā*) take up instructional assignments.

The mission of the Upanişads is not to lead one 'to know alone but through knowing to realize the non-duality of the finite and the infinite. Their reach, therefore, does not stop at the cognitive level which may produce insipid convictions and intellectual arrogance but takes in its ambit the entire being; cognitive, conative and affective in one sweep. Since the Brahma dwells within (antary*ā*min) the Ātman needs no search or reaching out but ought to be contemplated and meditated upon so that the illusory distinction of 'I' and 'Thou' disappears.

The characters of the parables and dialogues are so crafted that although they look as familiar as the neighbours next door, they retain the aura of being mythical, even mystic at times. These characters materialize on the scene precisely at an appointed time, play their respective parts gallantly and exit without ado in the manner of a puppet show. How life-like indeed! Some of them do make re-appearances in different contexts but most have gained immortality through a singular performance. The beauty is that the stage is never crowded and no one seeks limelight at the cost of the other.

And, now a couple of questions. First, how was I motivated to study the Upaniṣads? I do not know. All through the years with the Indian Army my field of endeavour comprised professional subjects like education, history and military history or at the most other social and behavioral sciences. But, as I hung up my uniform finally, I was led to this new path by an unknown but kindly light. Soon, it became a pursuit of intrinsic contentment and bliss. Second, why did I write these pages knowing well that a vast literature of value already exists on the subject? Briefly, on realization of the immense relevance of the Upaniṣadic philosophy of life in today's context, I came to believe that the teachings contained in these scriptures helped one in the process of self-actualization. I, therefore, felt an urge to share my understanding of the same with others, whatever the worth of my own convictions. This small volume has emerged in response to that urge. Through the pages that follow an effort has been made to offer a kind of intellectual appetizer to the readers so as to enhance their desire to partake the heavenly spread laid-on for them by the great masters elsewhere.

The parables and dialogues included in this work are only a few pearls collected at random from the great ocean of the Vedic lore. Of course, a vast wealth lies beyond them. Also, these few pieces do not, in any way, constitute a representative anthology, for each single brick of the great vedāntic edifice is its own class. Nevertheless, the present arrangement has shaped into a presentable bouquet, though of its own hue.

The book has been organized in two parts. The first part contains twelve parables which introduce the reader to some of the foundational postulates of the Upaniṣads. This part culminates with the exposition of one of the four Great Affirmations[4] of the Vedas viz. 'Thou That Are (Tat twam asi)'.

The second part of the book comprises five dialogues taken from the Muni Kānda (also known as the Yājńvalkya Kānda) of the Bṛhadāraṇykopaniṣad. These dialogues cumulatively establish the philosophy of Non-Duality (Advait), the acme of the Upaniṣadic instruction.

Each parable and dialogue included in this work is preceded by prolegomena and is followed by a brief comment. With a view to keeping the text racy citing of opinions has been avoided. But, explanations have been provided as and when the contexts so demanded. At places, some Sanskṛt expressions as transliterated in Roman script (with an approximate English equivalent placed in

---

[4] Each of the four Vedas has a Great Affirmation (Mahā vākya) about the Brahma. These are:-

Prajńānam Brahma; knowledge is Brahma: Ṛg Veda.

Aham Brahma Asmi; I am the Brahma: Yajurveda.

Tat Twam Asi; Thou That are: Sāma Veda.

Ayamātam Brahma: This self is Brahma: Atherva Veda

parenthesis) have been incorporated in the text. At other places, the Sanskṛt expressions have been placed in the parenthesis soon after the English version. This mode has helped in maintaining the momentum, clarity, and precision of thought.

Om Śāntiḥ Śāntiḥ Śāntiḥ

PART ONE

Chapter 1

The Divine Code of Virtuous Conduct

Prajāpati's Instruction to Gods, Humans and Demons

Prolegomena

Prajāpati[1], the Creator, is the father and preceptor of all beings. Since the gods, humans and the demons were all his children they often went to stay with him as seekers of

[1] The Creator God, as the first-born deity. He is the parent of all living and nonliving. The Prajāpati comprises five factors; father, mother, child, wealth and rites. The heaven, the sun and the mind are father, the earth, fire and organ of speech being his wife the mother; the vital breath is their child; the increasing-decreasing lunar cycles indicate wealth. Since these cycles are divisions of time they cause changes in the manifest world and represent rites. He is the First Person of the Hindu Trinity; the other two being Viṣṇu and Śiva.

Truth (Brahmachārins)[2]. On such occasions the father rather than administering long sermons or issuing edicts preferred to create an ambiance in which the seekers themselves discovered answers to their questions.

The Instruction

Once, the gods (devas) the humans (mānavas) and the demons (asuras) went to stay as seekers of true knowledge with their father, the Prajāpati. At the end of their stay, they approached the great preceptor for instruction. The gods were the firsts to come forward. Said they, "O' Venerable Sir, what discipline do you commend us to observe?"

Knowing that his wards were ready to receive instruction in right earnest, the Prajāpati said, "Da" and proceeded to ask.

"Do you understand what I mean?"

Spoke the gods, "Oh yes. By the letter 'da' you mean dama (restraint) and discipline you give us is 'Restrain Yourselves' (damayata) wherein you tell us that by nature we are given to sensuous pleasures and that we should take a better hold of our senses."

The Prajāpati said with satisfaction, "Yes, you do understand me correctly."

Then came the humans and asked the Prajāpati, 'O' Venerable Sir, what discipline do you commend us to observe?"

Replied the Prajāpati, "Da" and proceeded to ask," Do you understand what I mean?"

---

2 The brahmacharya-dharma was an essential part of the Code of Conduct laid down for all students staying at the hermitage of a teacher.

Said the humans, "Oh yes. By the letter 'da' you mean 'datta' (give) and the discipline you give us is to give in charity (dānam). You tell us that by nature we are misers and that we should share our bounties with others. Since this alone is in our best interest, nothing else could you be telling us".

Spoke the Prajāpati with satisfaction, "Yes. You do understand me correctly."

The demons were the last to reach. Said they, "O' father, what discipline do you commend us to observe?"

Said the Prajāpati, "Da". And proceeded too ask, "Do you understand what I mean?"

Replied the demons, "Oh yes. By the letter 'da' you mean 'dayā' (compassion) and the discipline you commend to us is 'be compassionate' (dayā-dharma). You tell us that by nature we are cruel and given to violence and that we should be compassionate toward all beings."

Spoke the Prajāpati with satisfaction, "yes, you do understand me correctly."

It is said; even today the afore-said divine teaching of the Prajāpati is proclaimed aloud by the thunder when it roars da-da-da to remind the triad discipline of self-restraint (dama), giving in charity (dāna) and compassion (dayā) as enjoined by the father to his progeny.

****

Let us understand as to who were the three types of seekers *viz.* the devas, the mānavas and the asuras.

The devas stand for those virtuous persons who also possess the material means and powers over others. They indeed are given to sensuous enjoyments. The mānavas are the common folk who remain involved in the humdrum of routine and are busy in acquiring the wherewithals needed for existence through fair means. And the asuras are the people who too like devas are given to sensuous living but who seek to obtain fulfillment of their desires by all means; fair and foul. So, the three types of Prajāpati's children do not belong to three different species. They indeed are the three segments of the same human community respectively representing on the scale of quality; the elite, the commonality and the baser elements. That is the societal angle to the issue.

On the individual plane, actions of each human being are at times prompted by sublime thoughts, at times guided by the run of the mill ideas and yet at other times directed by selfish and baser motives. Viewed so, each one of us is a deva, a mānava or an asura at some time or the other. That is the individual angle to the issue. Hence the need for a loud and clear reminder of the Instruction given by the creator to his progeny as summed up in simple terms of restraint, sharing and compassion.

How is it that the Creator ordained three different disciplines for the three different sets of learners? (All three disciplines had the same root, the letter 'da'). Herein is seen the divine nature of the instruction. During the period of stay of his wards at the hermitage the Prajāpati had created an opportunity for them to reflect deeply upon their respective weakness through self analysis which also led them to self instruction. Eventually, their self-awareness culminated into self realization. The gods realized that since they squandered away their wealth and power in pursuit of sensuous pleasures, though in fair manner, they faced defeats at the hands of demons times and again. The humans knew that an important reason of their misery was their attitude of non-sharing of their assets with their less fortunate brethren. For this reason, divided into classes and segments (the haves and the have-nots) they always remained either beholden to the gods or threatened by the devils. The demons, too, had realized that their tendency to succumb to passion and violence for fulfillment of desires resulted into frittering away of vital energies. Consequently, they were despised by the humans and kept under the thumb by the gods.

With the self-knowledge so welled up, all of them were waiting eagerly to know as to what solution their Father had to offer. The Prajāpati, of course knowing all this, struck right when the iron was hot.

We do experience in our lives as to how up-lifting it is to keep the senses under control, how rewarding it is to share possessions with the needy and how enervating it is to shun violence in thought and action.

Bṛhadāraṇykopaniṣad

Chapter 2

Who May He Be

The Yakşa Parable

Prolegomena

The Upanişads contain several stories concerning wars between gods (devas) and demons (asuras). One such story occurs in the Kenopanişad. The devas led by their king Indra represent the cosmic forces. In their subtle form they function also as the presiding deities of the corresponding senses of the human body. Of devas, Agni (the Fire), Vāyu (the Wind), Varuṇa (the Water) Suriya (the Sun) and Chandra (the Moon) are prominent. In the human body Agni is the deity of the eye, Vāyu that of the ear and so on. The asuras (the evil spirits) are the rivals of devas (the godly spirits). The two are in a perpetual conflict with each other for gaining primacy, both at the cosmic and individual levels.

The Parable

Once, in a battle, devas defeated their foes as was willed by the Supreme Being, the Brahma[1]. However, in their ignorance devas thought that the victory was all due to their own prowess. So, they believed the glory, too, was theirs. It is said that noticing their vanity and egoism the Brahma resolved to make devas aware of their limitations. Thus for their own good, the Supreme Being materialized in the form of a yakşa[2], dazzling in full glory where devas were celebrating their victory.

Blinded by ignorance and pride devas failed to recognize Him, wondering who could the non-challant and august visitor be. Scared in their hearts, for ignorance always breeds fear devas were keen to know as to 'Who He May Be'.

So, they asked the Fire-god to find out the identity of the visitor. Said they, "O' Omniscient, since you are the most glorious amongst us do go and recognize this yakşa who is dazzling our eyes and do particularly find out who he may be".

"So be it:" Said Agni. He went to the yakşa. Seeing him come as a seeker the August Being asked him, "Who you may be?"

"I am Agni, the consumer of all." Replied the fire god.

"Oh! If that be so, may I know as to what power you possess," asked the yakşa.

"I can reduce to ashes all there is in this world," boasted Agni.

---

1 When the demons triumph unrighteousness prevails but when gods win it is the virtue that flourishes. That was why the Supreme Being had willed the victory of the gods.

2 Yakşas are believed to be a class of celestial beings ranked just below the Devas in hierarchy.

The Brahma then placed a blade of grass before him and said, "Burn it O' Agni. Should you be unable to do so then forsake your claim as consumer of all?"

The fire god approached the blade of grass with all his heat and flame but could not even singe it. Realizing his limitation, Agni returned to his peers and admitted that the visitor was beyond his knowledge.

The devas then asked the Wind- god to approach the mighty visitor who had defied the omniscient Fire- god.

"So be it," said Vāyu before going to the dazzling visitor.

Knowing that the Wind- god was a seeker of truth the August Being asked him as to whom he was.

"I am Vāyu, the mātariśvā, the one who wanders about in the vast space unhindered," said the Wind-god.

"What powers have you?" asked He.

"I can sweep away in a whiff all that is there on the earth" replied Vāyu.

Then the yakşa placed a blade of grass before him and said, "Here you are mighty Vāyu, blow this blade you may."

The Wind-god approached the blade of grass with all his might but could not move it as much as a hair's breadth. In vain did he whirl and whang.

Dismayed Vāyu returned to his fellow gods wheezily and said, "He indeed is beyond my knowledge."

By then devas were indeed shaken as two of their powerful colleagues had failed to comprehend the intruder.

So, taking no more chances, they beseeched their king, Indra, to unravel the identity of the mighty visitor.

"So be it," said Indra.

Alas! The Supreme Being had disappeared even before Indra could reach Him.

Vainly had Indra believed that once in his presence he would know of the Unique Being.

The Lord verily had willed otherwise and gave Indra no such opportunity. There, of course, was no better way to make the king of gods aware of his limitations!

Lo and behold! Instead of the yakşa, Indra met at the spot an extremely charming lady gorgeously attired and bedecked with jewels. She was Umā, the daughter of the Himalayas, who like Pārvati was personified spiritual wisdom. With his pride vanished, Indra stood in silent wait like a true seeker of knowledge.

In all reverence, he spoke, "Pray, O' Mother tell me as to who might He be."

"This is Brahma' Said Umā. "In vain was your pride, O Indra, for the victory against the demons was His" she added.

It is said, at her words the revelation dawned and Indra came to know of the Brahma.

Since the Fire- god, the Wind -god and the king of gods had the unique opportunity of coming closer to Him, they enjoy a status of eminence among the gods. Also, since Indra was the first one to know that was Brahma, he is posited above all other devas. Verily, knowledge has primacy over simply seeing or talking to.

The Teaching

The seer of the parable has crafted this beautiful allegory with a dual purpose. On the spiritual plane, the parable alludes to the truth that through knowledge alone can one comprehend the glory of the Ātman, (the soul) or the Pramātman, (the Supreme Soul). The eyes cannot comprehend Him for He is the seer of the eye or the seeing itself and is the fire in the fire. Similarly, the ears cannot comprehend Him, for He is the hearer of the hearing itself.

If that be the case with the major sense-organs, the others like the smelling-nose or the touch for skin stand no chance of knowing Him. Even Indra, the lord of all other gods and master of all sense organs, could come to know Him only through pure intellect (buddhi) as personified by the Golden Umā in the parable. So is mentioned in the Smṛti, too: the God is known with the help of Vidyā. (Vidyā sahāya vāniśvara.)

On the mundane plane, the parable shows that the vices like pride, vanity and egoism, being the outcomes of ignorance, stand as impediments in the path of knowledge. Even the gods are prone to arrogance on attaining success. Unless these barriers of ignorance and arrogance are demolished with the help of Vidyā, Truth can not be seen in its resplendent glory. Moreover, no one can know the Truth unless it is revealed by some one who is pure. Through the words of Umā the revelation dawned and Indra came to perceive the Brahma.

Kenopaniṣad

Chapter 3

Deeds Sans Knowledge Earn Dishonour

The Parable of Uṣasti Chākrāyaṇa

Prolegomena

During the Vedic period, yajńas (sacrificial offerings) were deemed as deeds of great religious merit. So much so, that in almost every household a place (known as yajńa-śālā) was kept apart for performing yajńas. Initially, these rituals were quite simple and comprised reciting of chants and offering of oblations to gods through fire. Gradually, the rituals became complex and elaborate affairs conducted under a well defined and demanding code. For the purpose of understanding the present parable, it should suffice to know that a yajńa was conducted in three distinct stages *viz.* the introductory chants (the prastāva), the rising chants (the Udgitha) and the response chants (the Pratihārata). At each of these stages the prescribed chants were recited by a designated team of priests led by a headpriest.

The three head-priests worked under the supervision of the chief priest of the ritual. With the passage of time, the yajńas turned out to be expensive occasions as these were followed by giving of alms, exchange of costly gifts, and organiszing of feasts and festivities. Consequently, such rituals became a part and parcel of state ceremonials organized on behalf of the kings or lords of the realm or some rich people attracting learned priests from far and wide. Special attention was paid to the selection of priests to conduct a yajńa because as a rule the ritual could not be proceeded with if any one in the assembly raised a question with regard to the details of procedure and the issue was not settled by the priest to the satisfaction of all.

The Parable

Once, the land of Kurus experienced extreme famine conditions when the crops were destroyed by locusts or hailstorms.

(In such circumstances the priestly class, which lived on the offerings of food made to them by the householders always was hit the hardest.)

Even so, a well-known but young priest, Chākrāyaṇa Uşasti by name, roamed around along with his wife in search food. One day, they reached a village inhabited by elephant trainers. The sage duo obviously was very hungry and so they asked for alms at the house of one of the elephant trainers who were generally considered as untouchables. The embarrassed host told Uşasti, in all humility, that unfortunately he was left with only as much of beans as were already served in his plate to eat. He added that since he knew that a priest would not partake the left overs from any one's plate he had nothing to spare for alms. But, lo and behold! The priest agreed to share the left overs. The host, then gladly offered a portion of his food to the visitor. Uşasti Chākrāyaṇa ate only a part of the food and kept aside the rest for his wife who he believed was in a similar situation. Once the visitor had eaten some food, he regained enough strength to take leave of his benefactor. When the elephant man offered to share with him the drinking water, too, Uşasti refused to accept the same on the plea that he could not justifiably drink the left-over water. The quaint logic of the priest astonished the host who asked him as to how could he in that case justify eating of the left over food.

Uşasti explained his behaviour telling the elephant man that at the time of approaching his host for food he was almost at the verge of dying. The life, he said, was of prime importance and one was permitted to eat the otherwise uneatable to save oneself from dying. Since no food other than the left overs was available to him he justifiably ate the same. But, position had changed thereafter. Since he was no longer at the verge of dying for want of water which he could obtain from any other source, there was no justification for him to accept the left over water.

Having instructed the elephant man thus, the ṛşi[1] took leave of him and returned to his wife to give her food to

---

[1] The term 'rishi' or 'ṛşi' originally denoted the seers and singers of Vedic hymns. However, the rishi is also a sage to whom the God revealed the Vedas (knowledge of the eternal truths about the Creator, His creation and means to preserve it). The three chief classes of ṛşi are the Brahmaṛşi, born of the mind of Brahma, the Devaṛşi of lower ranking, and Rajaṛşi or kings who became ṛşi through their knowledge and austerities. The Shruta ṛşi are makers of Shastras, the Kandaṛşi are of the experts in conducting rituals. Saptaṛşi are two Sanskrit words joined together meaning 'Seven Sages'.

eat. The lady in the meantime had arranged for food on her own initiative. She therefore, kept the beans brought by her husband aside for later use.

Next morning, Uşasti informed his wife that a great yajńa was being performed at a king's place nearby for which services of many priests were being requisitioned. He lamented that if he had something to eat, he could muster strength to go to the king's yajńa-śālā to stake his claims for the office of the chief-priest. The good lady produced the beans she had saved the night before which both of them ate and reached their destination in time.

When the proceedings of the great ritual were about to commence with recitation of the introductory chants, Uşasti Chākrāyaṇa rose to his feet and asked the head priest of the team to tell the name of the deity that belonged to the chants. He warned that if the head-priest were to sing the prescribed chants without knowing the concerned deity his head would fall (Implying that he would earn dishonour). Pressing home his point ṛşi Chākrāyaṇa put similar questions successively to the heads of the teams which were respectively to recite the rising and the response chants and administrated a similar warning to them. Since the concerned priests did not know the names of the deities that belonged to their respective chants, a total silence descended upon the assembly. Dumb-founded the priests acknowledged the erudition of the young interlocutor.

The King, who by then had noticed the presence of the learned ṛşi, requested him to give out his identity. The visitor told the king that he was Chākrāyaṇa Uşasti that is Uşasti the son of the great ṛşi Chakra.

That was a pleasant surprise for the king who had made all efforts to trace Uşasti for the office of the Chief Priest of the ritual and had appointed some one else only when the ṛşi could not be located. The king invited Uşasti to take charge of the proceedings. The learned sage gladly accepted the offer on the condition that all priests whose services had already been requisitioned were also retained.

When the ritual was about to commence under the supervision of Uṣasti, the Prastotā Priests approached him to know as to who the deity of the introductory chants was. He told them that the Vital Breath (the Prāṇa) was the deity to whom their chants were addressed. "Verily", said he, "All living beings enter this world with breath and depart when the breath leaves them." Since they had now known the answer to his question, they could proceed with their chants without fear of incurring shame. Having satisfied themselves with the reply, the Prastotā Priests went back to their assigned places.

The Udgātā Priests were the next to come to Chākrāyaṇa. They said, O' Venerable sir, since we do not know as to what divinity belonged to the rising chants, kindly do tell us about him lest our heads fall when we sing the prescribed chants."

Replied Uṣasti, "Verily, the Sun (āditya) is the divinity that belongs to the rising chants. As is well-known, all living beings sing aloud in praise of the sun which is Omnipresent. You were wise to know it before commencing your chants otherwise your head would have hung in shame." Having satisfied themselves with the answer, the Udgata priests returned to their allotted places. There upon came the last batch of singers' *viz.* the Pratihārtas, who too inquired about the identity of the divinity that belonged to their chants.

"Food (anna) is the deity associated with the response or the concluding chants because all beings eat food as long as they live," Said Uṣasti. Having known the purpose of their chants, these priests, too, withdrew. Since there remained no more issues to settle the conduct of the yajńa proceeded smoothly there onward.

****

This is how Uşasti established a close relationship of yajńa with the vital breath, sun and food. Some Vedic commentators have opined that though put across differently, the expressions 'the prāṇa', 'āditya' and 'anna' stood for the Supreme Being or the Brahma only. They, therefore, say that the divinity associated with the yajńa all through is none else but the Supreme Being Itself.

Be that as it may, for obtaining a clearer understanding of the instruction of the parable both of its episodes ought to be viewed together. In the first episode that described the ṛşi's encounter with the elephant man is contained the key-thought of the instruction viz. life was of prime importance. All else is relevant to and is sustained by life only. One could earn merit so long as body and soul stayed together. The life as such is sustained by the energy provided for by the sun in relation to earth and by food in relation to body. These three, therefore, were the divinities that belonged to yajńa. The sage Uşasti practised whatever he preached. He accepted the otherwise prohibited food to keep him alive so that he could perform works of religious merit thereafter.

The parable has a great message to convey. Life is like a yajńa which is sustained by the bounties of nature like the air-energy, the sun-energy and the food-energy. These bounties must be held in all veneration as are held the three divinities associated with yajńa viz. the Vital Breath, the Sun and the Food. Such should be the conviction born of true knowledge. Needless to say, these days one encounters quite a few eco-priests who recite their prescribed chants for better environment without possessing abiding convictions with regard to the divine character of the elements of nature. Since these elements are sacred these have to be kept pollution free.

Viewed thus, Uṣasti Chākrāyaṇa's instruction is as much relevant today as it was during the hoary past.

Chhāndogyopaniṣad

Chapter 4

Primacy of the Vital Breath

Superiority of the Life Breath over other Breaths

Prolegomena

As per the Vedic belief, the human body is dependent on the soul (Ātmāśreya) for its existence and on the senses (Indriyāśreya) for its functioning. Since the senses provide vigour and momentum to the body, these are known also as its breaths (prāṇas). Primarily the body is acquired by the soul as its abode, but it (the body) also provides shelter to the senses. Thus, the body becomes the abode of the senses as well. In the common parlance, breath means the action of inhaling and exhaling of air (basically the oxygen which is vital for keeping the body cells alive), in the upanishadic discourse this aspect is understood as the Chief Breath, the primary sustainer of life. All the breaths (the sense-prāṇas, so to say) are important to the body individually as also collectively. Nevertheless, the breath that is vital and without which the other breaths have no existence has been referred to as the Vital Breath in this parable.

This parable examines the relative importance of the sense-breaths or the prāṇas vis-à-vis the vital breath or the mukhya prāṇa. The participating senses are the sense of seeing (chakşu), hearing, (śrotra), the speech (vāṇi) and the mind (manas) which respectively are quartered in the eye, ear, tongue and mind. The beauty of upanishadic perception is that it always proceeds from the gross to the subtle. So, wherever a particular sense is spoken of, the reference is made to the aggregate of its three aspects *viz.* its quarters or the body organ, its assigned ability and the power of divinity identified with it. For example, when the sense of seeing is mentioned, a simultaneous reference is made to the physical organ known as the eye, to the ability to see and to the divinity that enables the activity of seeing to take place. While it is easy to distinguish between the eye as an organ and its ability to see (there are many persons who possess eyes but are not able to see) but the distinction between the ability to see and the divinity identified with seeing is rather subtle. This latter difference can only be perceived and not demonstrated. A similar logic is applicable to all other senses as well.

Also, whatever is true about the infinitesimal self and the human body is correspondingly true in the context of the Infinite Self and the Cosmic Body of the Puruşa or the Supreme Being. In the cosmic context, fire (Agni), air (Vāyu), sun (surya/ āditya) and moon (Chandra) perform the functions of the senses of the Puruşa. These divinities also represent the three aspects *viz.* the heavenly bodies or elements as perceived, their respective abilities to perform the assigned roles and the divinities identified with each one of them. Thus, when we refer to fire, we simultaneously mean the flaming and blazing heat, its ability to consume and divinity of fire (the Fire-god). Same is true about the other cosmic forces functioning as the senses of the Puruṣa. All these forces or prāṇas of the cosmic body are important individually and collectively. There is however one force or breath without which all these other breaths have no existence. What power is that? That is what the ensuing parable purports to indicate or explain.

The senses (indriyas) are not merely the sources of information for the embodied self (jivātman), so to say. Instead, certain specific merits (guṇa) inhere in each one of them. For instance, the sense of speech (vāk) is the most prosperous and dominant (vaiśiṣtĥa) among them. He who possesses the facility of good and truthful speech has the potential to live in plenty and in a position of power and influence.

The sense of sight (chakṣu) keeps one steady while treading a level or an uneven ground. It obtains firmness and honour (Pratiṣtĥā). One, who possesses good ability to see, is obviously sure of oneself and has the potential to obtain glory. The sense of hearing (śrotra) alone enables one to know the Vedas and their meanings whereby one performs the prescribed works which, in turn, fulfil all desires in this world as also in the world beyond. So, the sense of hearing is the provider (sampadam). The mind is the abode (āyatan) of all thoughts and desires (viṣayas). All other senses also take refuge in mind only. One, who possesses a healthy and blemish-free mind, has the potential of generating good thoughts and thereby moving upwards in the human scale.

It is relevant here to perceive the difference between the two relative terms *viz.* the jyeṣtĥa (the eldest) and the śreṣtĥa (the superior most). While the former term denotes one's locus on the basis of age or time, the latter marks a locus in terms of merit or quality. Viewed thus the vital breath (mukhya prāṇa) is the eldest as it arrives first, right at the time of conception and is followed generally by the other senses, as the body grows. That is the jyeşt̂ha argument. This parable further establishes the superiority of the vital breath even on the śreşt̂ha or the qualitative argument.

The Parable

Once it so happened that each indriya (sense) claimed a position of superiority for itself over all others saying, "I am superior, I am superior." When they were not able to settle the dispute, they approached their father, the Creator (Prajāpati) and asked him as to who amongst them was the superior most.

Said the father, "He on whose leaving the body turns the worst is obviously the best."

On knowing this, the senses decided to leave the body one by one for a whole year. The speech (vāk) was the first one to leave. On return after an absence for a year, the speach found the business with the body going as usual. So it asked, "How could you all live without me for such a longtime?"

The others replied, "we lived as does the dumb not speaking but breathing with the breath seeing with the eyes, listening with the ears and thinking with the mind.' Realizing that it was not the most vital amongst them, the speech re-entered the body and resumed its functions.

Then, the sight (chakşu) departed from the body. Having stayed away for a year it returned only to fiind that nothing unusual had happened to the body. So, it asked, "Oh! How could you live without me for such a long time?"

Replied the others, "We lived as does the blind, not seeing, but breathing with the breath, listening with the ears, thinking with the mind and speaking with the tongue." The sense of sight realized that it surely was not the most vital amongst them. It re-entered the body and resumed its work.

The sense of hearing was the next to leave. Having stayed away for a year it returned only to find that no calamity had visited the body. In amazement it asked," Oh! How have you been living without me for such a longtime?"

Said the others, "We lived as does the deaf, not hearing but breathing with the breath, thinking with the mind, speaking with the tongue and seeing with the eyes." The sense of hearing then realized that it assuredly was not the most vital amongst them and entered the body to resume its work.

Thereafter the mind left the body boastfully. After gallivanting about for a whole year it returned only to find that all was well with the body. Asked he, "How come you could be still alive without me?" Said the others, "We lived as does a baby not thinking, but breathing with the breath, speaking with the tongue, seeing with the eyes and hearing with the ears." The mind then realized that it surely was not vital. Chastened so, it returned to the body and resumed its charge.

When the vital breath (the mukhya prāṇa) prepared to depart it was an altogether a different situation. In a hurricane like fury it destabilized the other senses the way a powerful horse, when hurt, tears off the pegs to which it is tethered. All other senses started feeling uneasy. Soon they came to the vital breath almost begging it not to leave. Together they said, most humbly, "O', venerable sir, you are our lord and master. You are superior to all of us. We pray thee; kindly do not depart from the body."

Said the speech,"If I am the most prosperous and dominant it is all because of you. Indeed, you alone are the prosperous and dominant one."

Said sight, "If I am the harbinger of firmness and honour it is all because of you. Indeed, you alone are the firm and honoured one."

Said hearing, "If I am the provider then it is all because of you. Indeed, you alone are the one who provides."

Said mind, "If I am the abode, then it is all because of you. Indeed, you alone are the abode."

****

The senses viz. speech, seeing, hearing and mind are known as life forces (prāṇas) because the vital breath, (the mukhya prāṇa) alone is all these forces perse. And, who is the vital breath (supreme sustainer, nay the sole sustainer) of the cosmos? Indeed, the Brahma alone is the vital breath of the cosmos.

Chapter 5

Pre-eminence of Air among Divinities

The Parable of Raikwa, the man with a cart

Prolegomena

In chapter-4 above, primacy of the vital breath vis-à-vis other life forces has been established. The Upanishad through the parable that follows has re-established the same truth from another stand point. This parable has two characters; one is a king called Jānaśruti and the other a learned man named Raikwa. The sage Raikwa lived in a remote village but was widely known for his deep learning and piety. Since he always travelled in a cart driven by a horse, he was known by his epithet of 'the man with a cart'. Jānaśruti too was a meritorious and popular king of his time. Interestingly, both these characters are introduced to the reader by a pair of swans.

The Parable

Once there was a king named Jānaśruti who was known for his liberality in giving alms and offering food. For purpose of charity, he had got rest houses constructed along the highways of his kingdom where travellers could stay and have food free of cost. It so transpired that one evening when the king was taking rest atop his palace a pair of swans happened to fly over. As the swans were about to approach the king's palace, the one flying behind the other cautioned his mate saying, "O' you, the short-sighted one! Don't you see the blazing shaft of light issuing forth from the meritorious works of King Jānaśruti rising up in the sky? I beseech, you avoid flying over there lest you should burn to ashes".

The leading swan retorted, "Oh! I am amazed; you talk in such laudable terms about this despised and lowly king as if you were talking about the sage Raikwa, the man with a cart." Said the former, "Kindly tell me more about the person about whom you speak in such high praise." The leading swan replied, "I vouch, as all the lower throws in the game of dice go to the highest thrower, so do all the good things that the people do go to Raikwa. Whoever knows what he knows?" (This meant that the merit and knowledge of Raikwa were unrivalled)

The king, who had overheard the conversation between the swans, was taken aback. He called his personal attendant and expressed his desire to meet Raikwa, the man with a cart. On receiving the king's directions the attendant proceeded to locate the sage. Alas! He returned to the palace only to tell the king that Raikwa could not be found. Obviously, the attendant had looked for the learned man among other cartmen. He was then directed by Jānaśruti to look for him where the wise men lived. Verily, the attendant found the wise man resting under a Cart.

"Are you, sir, the famous Raikwa?" asked the king's attendant.

'Yes, assuredly, I am." Replied the man.

The attendant returned to the palace post haste and broke the good news to the king.

The king collected some six hundred milk-yielding cows, a precious necklace and a fine chariot drawn by young she-mules (aśvatriratham) as gifts for Raikwa and reached the sage's residence. After the gifts had been laid out, the king spoke, "O' venerable sir, please accept these gifts and instruct me about the deity on whom you meditate." (During the Vedic period learned teachers imparted instruction only to such seekers who approached them with humility and faith, showing submission, care and good conduct. The rich and expensive gifts did not lure the true teachers. Nevertheless, by tradition suitable gifts were offered by the house-holders to their teachers as a mark of respect. It seems, in this case the king was not sufficiently respectful in his approach.) Replied Raikwa, "Oh! The chariot, the necklace and the cows, all these you keep to yourself, you śudra!"

(The question here arises as to why should a learned man like Raikwa address a king like Jānaśruti in such a derogatory manner. Śankarāchārya provides a clarification. Says the great teacher, "the teachers quite often address their students as 'O you donkey', 'O you bull' when the latter do something foolish or stupid. Similarly, the sage Raikwa used the expression 'O, You śudra' for Jānaśruti even when he actually was not a śudra. Raikwa had come to know what all was passing through his visitor's mind, who was jealous of the sage's knowledge and reputation, as he had come after getting stumped up by the swans. Anyone who had such lowly feelings for his preceptor deserved to be rebuked. Perhaps, Raikwa also had felt that the gifts offered by the king were not befitting his (the king's) status or the social standing of the sage himself. All the same, the king got the message right and returned to his palace with his retinue and the gifts.)

After some time, Jānaśruti returned to the hermitage of Raikwa with as many as one thousand cows, a necklace, the chariot deriven by she-mules and his young daughter. Then he said, "O' Raikwa, here are a thousand cows, a necklace, a chariot driven by the she-mules and my daughter as your bride. Also, I present to you this village in which you live. Pray sir, instruct me on the deity you meditate upon," Looking at the face of the king's daughter, Raikwa said "All these cows and gifts are all right but O' śudra, this beautiful face was enough for you to make me speak," Thereafter, that village in the Province of Mahāvṛśās was called the Raikwa Parna. The sage then, proceeded to impart instruction to the king.

(It would seem odd to the modern reader that a person who was reputed to be the knower of Brahma, should accept a young girl as a gift and that an equally knowledgeable king should so gift away his daughter. Rightly or wrongly, even today in a traditional Vedic marriage a father gives his daughter away as a gift to his son-in-law, who in the presence of all, including gods, accepts her as such. But the ceremony is complete only once the bride and the groom accept each other on terms of equal partnership. Is there a better way for a father to give his daughter away in marriage?

Generally readers measure the ethical value of a statement or an episode on the scales of acceptance of their own times rather than on the norms prevailing during the times when the statement in question was made or the said episode had been constructed as an instructional encounter.

Needless to say, the Upanishads were recorded in the language and idiom as per the societal ethos prevailing at the place of their origin some thousands of years ago. Thus, these lores are contextual in their form but assuredly these texts are universal and time enduring in their instruction.)

The sage began his instruction thus: "Verily, the air (Vāyu) alone is the assimilator (samvarga) of all or the absorber of all. When the fire gets extinguished it gets embosomed into air, when the sun sets, it (the sunness) gets embosomed into air, when the moon sets, it (the moonness) gets embosomed into air, when the water dries up it gets assimilated in the air because air alone is the absorber of all of them *viz.* the fire, the sun, the moon and the water. So much is said about the assimilation of the concerning divinities (the cosmic forces)."

"And now are taken up the matters concerning the self (ātman). The life-breath (prāṇa) alone is the assimilator of all. When one goes to sleep, the speech (vāk) gets embosomed into the life breath, the sight (chakşuaḥ) gets embosomed into the life-breath, the hearing (śrotram) gets embosomed into the life breath, the mind (manaḥ) gets embosomed into the life breath because the life breath alone is the absorber of all these senses (indriyas)".

Then he concludes:

"Verily, these two are the only assimilators: Among the divinities it goes by the name of air (Vāyu) and among the senses, it is known as the life breath (prāṇa)".

****

In fact, Vāyu and prāṇa is one and the same thing. The distinction here is made only to highlight the two aspects of the Brahma viz. being the cosmic force for the Creation as Vāyu and the life force for the body as prāṇa.

Otherwise as well, Vāyu and prāṇa both are indicative of Brahma. Vāyu is the provider of motion to all (sarvesām gatipradam), an attribute of God. Being the essence of life, Prāṇa also is an attribute of God. The teaching, therefore, is that one should meditate on God or Brahma alone and not on other divinities.

At this juncture, a question may arise as to how come 'air' has been accorded the status of the supreme divinity when it is well known that Indra is the chief of all divine forces (Chapter-1 above). The answer has been provided in the Bṛhadāraṇykopaniṣad (1-5-21,22), where it has been stated that whereas all other divinities like the sun, the moon, the fire and the water disappear at one time or the other, the air is ever and omnipresent. Hence it's pre-eminence. Also, since allegorically Vāyu means God (Prameśwara), it is the supreme deity.

Chhāndogyopaniṣad

Chapter 6

Nature A Great Educator

The Parable of Satyakāma Jābāl

Prolegomena

The Indian philosophical literature is full of analogies and parallelisms which are used for explaining complex thought and unfolding mysteries. This parable from Chhāndogya Upanişad explains the all-pervading nature of Brahma as told to a young seeker by a team of teachers in a forest. These educators comprised a bull (ŗşabha), the fire (Agni), a swan (hamsa) and a diver-bird (mudgu).

During the Vedic period children on attaining a certain age were initiated for education through a formal ceremony, known as the Upanayana Samskāra. The student candidate at this stage had full freedom to choose his teacher. For this purpose he could approach a head of an academy (āchārya) either by going to him alone or accompanied by his father. A rigorous interview always followed such a request in which a variety of questions were asked from the suppliant pertaining to his parentage and socio-cultural background so as to assess his motivation level, aptitudes, intelligence level and the nature of general exposure. On such an assessment depended the allocation of a specific course of study, the period of stay at the academy as also the selection of the specific method of instruction. Having satisfied himself about the learner in all aspects did the āchārya accord approval for admission, Thereupon the life-long teacher – disciple (guru-śişya) relationships were literally initiated through fire by performing a yajńa (sacrificial fire) for which the young initiate contributed the fire wood collected from the forest.

For a clear understanding of this parable another point to take note of is about the way people adopted surnames in ancient India. Generally, one was known by his patrimonial family name called the gotra. But at times surnames were acquired from mothers, too. Such occasions, however, were rare and catered for certain contingencies. For instance, if a man had more than one wife, his children were known by the name of their respective mothers just as king Dasratha's son Laksmaņa was known as Soumitra (son of queen Sumitrā) and the legendary Bhişma was known as Gangā-Putra (son of Gangā). One was also known after his mother if father's identity was not known. The hero of this parable was one Satyakāma Jābāl (the son of a lady called Jabālā) and the preceptor to whom he went for his initiation ceremony was a famous academician called Gautama Hāridrumata that is the son of ŗşi Haridrumata born in the Gautama gotra.

In this work, focus so far has been on gaining understanding of the divine forces at work in the cosmos and their relationship with the life sustaining forces in the human body. One of the unique and great philosophical discoveries of the vedic thinkers was the postulation that whatever existed in the Cosmos or the macrocosm, existed in the body (the human body) or the microcosm. This invaluable formulation made the understanding of the relationship between the Creater and the Creation a great deal more comprehensible. During the course of delebrations in the previous chapters we learnt that as breath is vital for the body so is the Breath vital to the Cosmic Body; the Puruṣa. Indeed both these breaths being the same viz. the Ātman or the Brahma. Obviously, one would be keen to know a bit more about the Puruṣa, at least to the extent that could be related to the manifest reality. This precisely is the theme of this discourse.

[The term Ātman denotes the ultimate reality, omniscient, all powerful, free from all phenomenal characteristics such as hunger and thirst, eternal, pure, illumined, free, unborn, un-decaying, deathless, immortal, fearless and non-dual. (Śankarāchārya). As per the non-dualistic philosophy (Advait) the Ātman (Supreme Soul) and the ātman (individual soul) are the same.]

The Parable

Once there lived a lady called Jabālā, who had a son named Satyakāma. When the boy came of age he expressed desire to his mother to commence his education for which he wanted to go to a āchāryakul (an academy). Since a candidate for the initiation ceremony was required to be aware of paternal lineage (kulagotra), Satyakāma inquired about it from his mother.

His mother said, "I know not O' dear son, about your gotra. In my youth when I got you I was employed as a maid by several persons. Nevertheless, my name is Jabālā and your's Satyakāma. In case the āchārya asks you about your gotra, tell him that assuredly you are Satyakāma Jābāl." The young lad chose to go for his studies to the āchāryakul headed by ṛṣi Hāridrumata and told the āchārya about the purpose of his visit. When he was questioned about his gotra Satyakāma truthfully stated, "O'Venerable one, this I do not know. Before commencing the journey to your academy I had inquired about it from my mother and she told me thus, 'Going about a great deal as a maid servant during my youth I got you. So I do not know what gotra you belong to. Nevertheless I am Jabālā and you are Satyakāma. In case the āchārya asks you about your gotra tell him that assuredly you are Satyakāma Jābāl." To this, the āchārya said, "O, dear, No one but a Brāhmin can speak so candidly. You have not forsaken the path of truth. Go and fetch the fire wood, I shall initiate you".

After the ceremonies were over, the guru took out as many as four hundred weak and lean cows from his pen which he handed over to Satyakāma and said. "Go ye O' Satyakāma to the forest along with these cows". Accepting the assignmwent the lad promised to his master that he would take good care of his charge and that he would return to the hermitage only when the number of cows swelled to a thousand. He stayed in the forest for several years tending the cows well. One day, when the number of cows grew to a thousand the bull in the herd spoke, "O' you gentle Satyakāma, we are now one thousand. Would you be kind enough to take us back to hermitage? In the meantime, however, if you are keen to know I may tell you about one foot of the Brahma. "O' Respectable one, do kindly enlighten me so" Replied Satyakāma.

The bull said, "The first part of this foot is the east, the west is the second, the south is the third and the north is the fourth part. This four-part foot (chatuṣkal-pad) of the Brahma is known as the 'Illumined one' (prākāśwān). He who understands this four-part foot of the Infinite thus, becomes illumined himself and through such knowledge comes to know of other illumined worlds, too. Then the bull told Satyakāma that instruction about the second foot of the Brahma will be imparted to him by fire (agni).

Next day, the youngman collected his herd and started off towards the āchāryakul. Enroute when the evening fell he spotted a suitable place for the night halt. Having penned the cows safely, he lit a bonfire and sat down close to it facing eastword. Suddenly, he heard the fire calling him out "O' Satyakāma! In case you are keen to know, I may tell you about the other foot of the Brahma." Satyakāma said, "O Respected one, please enlighten me so".

Spoke the fire, "The first part of this foot is earth (pṛthvi), the second is space (antarikşa) the third is the world of light (diyu-lok) and the fourth is the ocean (samudra). Assuredly, the name of this four-part foot of the Brahma is Endless (Anantwān). He who understands this four-part foot of the infinite becomes endless himself and through such knowledge acquires endless worlds. O' Satyakāma the swan will impart instruction to you about the other foot of the Brahma". Saying so, the fire departed.

Next morning the youngman collected his herd and started off in the direction of the āchāryakul. When the night fell, he put the cows in a pen safely, lit a bonfire and sat down close to it facing eastward. Suddenly, he heard a swan calling out for him, "O' Satyakāma, in case you are keen to know, I may tell you about the other foot of the Brahma." Satyakāma requested, "O' Respectable one, kindly do enlighten me so."

Spoke the swan, "one part of the third foot of the Brahma is the fire (Agni), the second is the sun (Suriya), the third is the moon (Chandra) and the lightning (Vidyut) is the fourth part. This four-part foot of the Brahma is known as luminous (Jyotiśmān). He who understands this four-part foot of the infinite thus becomes luminous himself in this world and through such knowledge acquires the luminous worlds. O' Satyakāma, the instruction about the other foot of the Brahma will be imparted to you by the diver-bird (mudgu). Saying so, the swan flew away.

Next morning the youngman collected his herd as usual and started off in the direction of the āchāryakul. When the night fell, he put the cows in a pen safely, lit a bonfire and sat down close to it facing eastward. Suddenly, he heard a diver bird calling out for him, "O' Satyakāma, in case you are keen to know, I may tell you about the other foot of the Brahma". Requested Satyakāma, "O' Respected one, kindly do enlighten me so."

Spoke the diver-bird, "The first part of this foot of the Brahma is the life-breath, (prāṇa) the second is the eye (chakṣu), the third is the ear (śrotra) and the fourth is the mind (manas). The name of this four-part foot is Quarters (āyatanwān). He who meditates on this four-part foot of the infinite himself becomes the possessor of quarters in this world and through such knowledge comes to possess other worlds of such quarters". Saying so, the diver bird flew away.

Satyakāma returned to the āchāryakul along with the herd. Ṛṣi Gautama was very happy to receive him. After handing over the cows and paying of greetings the young disciple asked his guru what his further orders were.

Spoke the āchārya, "O' you gentle and well-mannered Satyakāma! Your face is lit like that of a knower of Brahma. O' dear, who has instructed you in this discipline? Assuredly, the radiance on your face tells me that you have been so instructed."

Replied Satyakāma, "O, Venerable one! Yes, though some one other than human. But, I request you to instruct me on the subject as and when you so desire because I have come to know from the āchāryas like you that the knowledge received from a guru alone leads one on to the path of ultimate goodness. Kindly do educate me in the knowledge about the infinite."

Thereafter, the learned sage taught Satyakāma all about the Brahma.

Comments

The parable has two messages to convey. Firstly, it demonstrates that the nature by itself is a great educator. All the objects of nature whether animate or inanimate are open books where from knowledge may be acquired ranging from the gross to the subtle. What matters more is the motivation of the seeker to receive the right message and contemplate upon it. Once the true desire is kindled even an instructional encounter with a bull or a diver bird becomes richly meaningful, rewarding and blissful. The scriptures have proclaimed aloud that 'Let good thoughts come from all directions.' It is the message and not the messanger that matters. All the same, need for a human guide, the guru, is paramount for he not only knows but also has the ability to communicate and guide the seeker in the light of his own personal experiences. Secondly, this parable conveys a social message of immense significance. Satyakāma was not born out of a socially recognized or lawful wedlock. But his mother had provided for sound foundations of truth and sincerity to his personality which is so important for a guilt and complex free life. Consequently, even the uncertain parental lineage was no hindrance in his personal development.

It is worth a mention that in due course of time Satyakāma rose to become one of the very well known philosophical thinkers of his time. Although substantial credit for all that must go to his sage-preceptor Gautama

Hāridrumata and the prevailing system of education, yet the major piece of the cake goes to Jabālā, the lady who in turn has been immortalized through this parable.

Chhāndogyopaniṣad

Chapter 7

What after Death?

Nachiketā's Dialogue with Death

Prolegomena

The parable of Nachiketā is the story of the Kat͡hopaniṣad. The same story is told in the Taittiriya Brāhmaṇa also, with only a marginal difference towards the end. In the story below, the Kat͡ha version has been followed. The Kat͡hopaniṣad is euologised widely both for its philosoply and linguistic excellence. Introduced to the European scholars by Rājā Rām Mohan Roy, Kat͡ha has been translated in several languagues. Several commentaries and scholarly glosses on this Upaniṣad also have been published.

The poser what after death has agitated the mankind always and everywhere. Perhaps its linkage whith the perception of 'reward and punishment' has made it the concern of every individual. The 'fear of the unknown' too has been a major prodding force to impel the sage and the devil alike to brood over this issue. The Kat͡hopaniṣad presents a very potent argument on the subject from the proverbial horse's mouth viz. the Lord of Death.

The Parable

Once, a Brāhmin Vājaśravā by name vowed to give away all his possessions as gifts after a yajńa so as to earn glory in this world and merit for the world yonder. When the gifts were being apportioned for the priests at the end of the yajńa he was left only with some old and barren cows. His son Nachiketā, a perceptive young lad who was watching all this felt that the gifting of such cows to the priests was not in the interest of his father. He mused, 'The man who after a yajńa gave cows in gift which gave no milk and which were unable to multiply further would go to the world of sorrow after death.' And such a situation he could not accept for this father. He was well aware that nothing else was left in the house which could be given away to the priests for their diligent performance of the yajńa nor could they be sent empty handed.

In a childlike manner, he reckoned that something valuable was still left with his father which could replace the old cows. And that valuable possession of Vājaśravā was Nachiketā himself. So, he asked his father, "O' father, to whom are you giving me?" Since the oldman was busy with important affairs, he paid no heed to his son's question. When Nachiketā kept on repeating the question, his father obviously lost his cool. May be that he himself was none too happy to give away such poor gifts to the deserving priests. In a fit of anger Vājaśravā declaimed, "To Yama, the Lord of Death, do I give you."

It was easier said than done. But young Nachiketā took it seriously and submitted that since he was neither a bad son nor a bad student his father ought to have some specific purpose in mind while making such a choice. So, he left for the abode of the Yama.

It so happened that when Nachiketā reached Yama's palace, the latter was out on a visit. So, the boy had to wait at the door-steps of Death for three days without food. When the Lord of Death returned, he was informed by his wife and ministers that a Brāhmin visitor was waiting or him. Of course, Nachiketā was not among the usual visitors to the Abode of Death who came there at the end of their time. Instead, he had arrived there in pursuance to the resolution (sankalpam) of his father made at the end of a meritorious religious ritual. So, Yama was obliged to offer him the traditional hospitalities due to a Brāhmin visitor as enjoined in the Law.

On meeting Nackiketa, Yama was impressed by the composure of the young man and granted him three boons as compensation for his going without food for three nights. Said Nachiketā, "O' Death, grant me as one of my boons that my father Vājaśravā becomes well disposed towards me, void of all anger and totally at peace so that when you return me to him he recognizes me and talks to me as my dear old father," (That he asked the boon for the happiness of his father, speaks very high of his moral fibre.) The Lord of Death granted the boon.

"O' Death, there is no fear in the heaven whatsoever. Even thou have no power out there. No one fears old age. Nor does anyone suffer hunger or thirst. All enjoy bliss, with no griefs to worry about. Since you know the great fire that carries the virtuous beings to heaven, be kind enough to tell me about that. This is my second boon." Said Nachiketā.

"O' Nachiketā, verily I know about that fire[1] and I shall share that knowledge with you. Be it known, that fire resides in the minds and hearts of the intelligent people.

---

1 Obviously, the great fire about which Nachiketā wanted to know was not the common fire known to humans. The issue had wider, deeper and subtler significance. As is commonly said, one is fired

"Such a fire though resides within, it has to be lit thrice a day under the guidance of one's three teachers' *viz.* the father, the mother and the āchārya" Lord Yama told Nachiketā.

Then, Yama provided Nachiketā with the secret knowledge of the sacrificial fire in question and the procedure for performing the concerned ritual which the lad understood well. Happy with the good uptake of the young learner Yama said. "You are the first mortal to know about this fire O' Nachiketā. Hereafter this fire will be known after your name.[2] This I grant you as an additional boon". He, who knows the Nachiketā fires and propitiates it with this knowledge, gets rid of the shackles of death, goes beyond sorrow and enjoys the bliss of heaven.

"O' Nachiketā, now you ask for the third boon,

Spoke Nachiketā, "Some say that after death the deceased exists, others deny it. Tell me the truth regarding this mystery. O'Lord"[3].

---

with noble ideals of charity, sacrifice and learning which denote an intense desire to do such deeds. Nachiketā was referring to such a fire.

2 This fire is also known as 'The Triple Fold Fire'- Triṇāchiketa. Its three constituents are performance of sacrifices (Yajńa), study of scriptures (Svādhyāya) and giving of alms (dānam). The message of the Upaniṣad is that one who during one's life time puts to fire all his works motivated by non-purificatory and irreligious activity, non – knowledge and the actions prompted by desires and feeling of ill-will towards others, on departing from this world leaves behind all the pain and grief and proceeds to enjoy the bliss and tranquility of the heaven.

3 Nachiketā now proceeds towards his main aim. As an obedient son it was his first duty to ensure that the anxieties and anger of

Taken aback, Yama tried to persuade the boy not to ask for such a subtle and difficult to comprehend knowledge, of which even the gods did not have clear perception. Such a statement from Yama, however, whetted the curiosity of the young mind further and Nachiketā insisted on obtaining this knowledge in preference to the much coveted gifts, which the Lord of Death offered to him in lieu. He was not a lad of common ilk and therefore, he could neither be enticed by attractions of the flesh nor could his steadfastness be shaken through persuasion or imploring. His mind was made up. After all, he had dared all odds and confronted the mighty death itself. He did not want to squander away his chance for transitory rewards, whatever was their worth. Once Yama was satisfied that the boy was worthy of receiving the subtle knowledge he granted him the boon, as desired.

Said he, "If you so insist O' Nachiketā, then listen what I say. There are two paths open to a person during his life; one of śreya or science (vidyā) and the other of preya or nescience (avidyā). The former path leads to immortality while the latter caters for worldly achievements, glories and pleasures. Although both of these objectives (goals of the two paths) may take recourse to the well-being of others, by their inherent nature the two paths are posited against each other. The path of śreya is difficult to follow but the

---

his father were taken care of. That explains his first boon. Then, he had seen yajńas being performed by people everyday, many a time for attainment of heaven. Since he wanted to know about the nature of the ritual, he asked for the second boon. All the same, his main objective was to acquire that particular knowledge which the Lord of Death alone was competent to provide with authority. And, he did not want to miss the opportunity of achieving his aim. Hence the third boon *viz.* what happens after death?

path of preya is easier and attractive. Remember, the wise-men (who are rare to be found) choose the path of śreya and those who are stupid select the path of preya. The persons falling into the latter category, being deluded, selfish and blind about reality see nothing beyond death and come to me time and again."

Yama then taught Nachiketā all about the science of yoga, the process through which the joys and sorrows of the world are forsaken leading one to the world of the Supreme Being. He also instructed him on the mystic word, 'Aum" which is the symbol of the Supreme Being. Eventually, Yama took up the theme of immortality of the self (ātmā).

Said Lord Yama, "The self neither is born nor does it die. It is born of no cause, nor has it evolved from some form of its own. It is eternal, primeval and constant. Since non-eternal things alone decay the eternal self can neither be slain nor does it otherwise decay. The self is all-pervading consciousness and is smaller than the smallest and greater than the greatest. It stays in the cavity of the heart of all beings including the gods. All things that have names and forms are only the limitations or the identities of the Self alone.

"On so realizing, the wise men leave all sorrow behind and believe 'I am This.' Such a self cannot be reached through ordinary knowledge or instruction. Nor can it be attained by reading the scriptures or by way of listening to sermons and discourses alone. He who seeks to know the self for the sake of self alone can know it through self itself[4].

---

4 That is to say, no external knowledge can lead one to the realization of the self. The self alone can reveal itself to a true seeker.

"He who has not cast off the effects of his evil-works (karmas), whose senses (indriyas) are not at peace and whose mind is turbulent and unstable can not reach the self even if such a person knows about the self."[5]

Nachikata's question, however, still remained unanswered. Yama had yet not told him as to what happened to the soul after death. To explain this subtle issue Yama used a beautiful simile. Said he, "Take the body as a chariot, the soul as the rider of the chariot, the intellect as the charioteer and the mind the reins.

Those who know, call the senses the horses and the pathways that these horses take, the objects (vişayas). This self which is embodied and is in possession of mind and the senses is called by the wisemen as 'the enjoyer' (bhoktā). As a competent driver who possesses a well-balanced intellect keeping an effective control over his fine horses takes them on to the right path even so does a person of understanding, of good conduct and of pure mind who keeping an effective control over his senses reaches the Brahma from where one returns no more. On the other hand, like a chariot driver who is incompetent and is of unstable and impure mind is unable to take his horses on to the right path even so does a person of false understanding and impure mind who having no control over his senses remains involved in the chain of life and death.

---

[5] From the stand-point of the effects of karamas (Karmabhog) there are two levels of soul. One is the individual soul which is infinitesimal (immeasurably small) and is the essence of all that has name and form. It is subject to re-brith. The other is Universal Soul which is infinite (immeasurably great) which is not affected by the works. The latter is the light and the former is its shadow. The two are inseparable and so they verily are one only.

"Know ye O' Nachiketā that higher than the senses are the objects of these senses and higher than these objects is the mind. The intellect is higher than the mind and the cosmic intelligence (Mahān-ātmā) is superior to the individual intellect. Higher than the cosmic intelligence is the un-manifest (Avyakta-Prakṛti). The Person (the Puruṣa) is superior to the un-manifest and there is nothing higher than or superior to the Puruṣa. He is the ultimate goal. The Puruṣa, so stated, includes the individual infinitesimal self as also the Infinite Self. The self as such is immanent and yet it does not shine or sparkle in the worldly sense. Only those who possess a subtle intellect, which is capable of seeing the subtle, are able to know It or see It. All this is not an easy task. Those who know the reality find the path sharper than a razor's edge and extremely difficult to follow."

Having thus established the glory of the self, Yama exhorted, "Arise and awake from the slumber of ignorance[6] and go ye to obtain the true knowledge from worthy preceptors. The true knowledge is very subtle and is an object of a worthy and subtle intellect alone. Those who so know alone can guide you on to the path of true understanding."

And what is the nature of this knowledge which is most worthy of knowing?

---

6 Ignorance denotes obscuring of the vision of Reality. At a higher level it means diverse knowledge and superimposition (māyā). The term māyā is a unique concept of the ancient Indian philosophy. It is the cosmic illusion on account of which the non-dual appears to be dual, the absolute appears as the relative existence and the one appears to become another like the desert seen as mirage and the rope appearing as snake, as it were.

Yama elaborated, "This world ever remains under the spell of the five senses viz. the speech, the touch, the form (seeing), the taste and the smell. So it is manifest. Similar is the case with this body, which also remains under the spell of the same senses. So, it is perishable. But there exists a subtle integration among all fundamental elements. Such an integrated whole is great, pure, constant and yet without adverse effects of the objects of senses. He who comes to know of the Being, who is soundless, touchless, formless imperishable, tasteless, odorless, constant, without a beginning and without an end, stable and higher than the highest, is liberated from the jaws of death. O' Nachiketā, the only way to know Him is through yoga *viz.* merging of the objects of the senses in the mind, merging of the mind in the individual intellect and finally merging all this in the Supreme Being. By doing so, one becomes free from nescience (avidyā), desire (kāma) and works (karmas) which are nothing but forms of death itself."

Since Nachiketā had obtained the true knowledge from a great preceptor like Yama in the true spirit of a seeker, he became immortal, free form the cycle of births and deaths.

Thus ends the parable of Nachiketā.

The message of the parable is that one who prefers to follow the path of sensual gratification over the path of meritorious living hankers after the worldly pleasures all the while running from pillar to post believing them to be the reality. Such a person is unable to perceive and realize that unifying principle by which ultimately all beings merge into the Supreme Being. As a consequence, such an unperceiving person meets death after death transmigrating from one body to the other as per his actions and earned merit. On the other hand, the one who acquires this knowledge of the ultimate unity in the so-seen diversity in the manifest and the non-manifest through the practice of yoga becomes the Brahma Himself, just as a drop of pure water merging into the ocean of purity itself becomes such an ocean. And from there, there is no come back.

Kathopnisad.

Chapter 8

The Cycle Of Deaths And Births

The Panchāgni Instruction

Prolegomena

There are three characters in this parable namely Āruṇi Gautama, a learned house-holder, his son Śvetketu and a philosopher king Pravāhaṇa Jaivali. Āruṇi was a scion of the famed Ṛṣi Aruṇa. It seems, Aruṇa was the name of a clan of the early Aryans whose complexion was reddish like the shade that spreads over the horizon at the break of the dawn. Even though this clan does not exist today as a separate identity, the name Aruṇa has retained a common fancy. So being the son of Aruṇa the boy Śvetketu was called Āruṇeya. The name Śvetketu, which literally means the one whose reputation is spotlessly white, appears in the Vedic literature at several places. Similarly, the name of the king also is suggestive of his being a person enjoying high esteem. Pravāhaṇa literally means the one whose sense-competencies are of a high order. Thus, we are introduced to a fine combination of characters viz. a knowledgeable father, an intelligent young learner and a philosopher king.

The parable unfolds at the court of the king where learned people are assembled for a religious discourse.

The Parable

Once, a descendent of Ṛṣi Aruṇa, Āruṇeya Śvetketu by name went to participate in religious discourses at the assembly of the Province of Pānchāla which were organized by its king Pravāhaṇa Jaivali. Noticing a new participant, the king asked the youngman if he was adequately instructed by his father before permitting to come to the Pānchāla Assembly.

By a tradition prevalent during the Vedic period, it was the responsibility of a father to impart adequate instruction in religious lore to his offsprings before sponsoring them to the assemblies of learned people. Obviously, Śvetketu answered in affirmative. At that point of time, the assembly happened to be discussing the question of what after death. So, with a view to testing the subject knowledge of the young participant the king asked, "O' youngman, do you know where people go to after death?'

"No, I do not know this, O' Venerable one". Replied Śvetketu.

"Do you know as to how do they come back?" Asked the king.

"I do not know this either". Śvetketu stated respectfully.

"How is it that so many people die and go to the yonder world but that place does not get filled up?" was the third question put by king Jaivali.

"That too I do not know, O' King", said Āruṇeya. The king then asked the fourth question, "Do you know where do the paths leading to the world of gods and to the world of fathers- the paths which are respectively known as the Devayāna and the Pitṛyāna separate?"

"No. O' Venerable one" Replied the bewildered Śvetketu. Then the king asked the fifth and the final question, "Do you know as to how in the fifth oblation, water is known as person?" "No, Sir," replied the youngman.

Obviously, the king was unhappy to receive all the answers in negative. He scolded Śvetketu saying, "How do you, O' youngman, claim that you have been adequately instructed? No one who is unable to answer these questions can claim to have been so instructed." Śvetketu felt embarrassed and retuned home post haste, even declining the offer made by the king for his stay in Pānchāla for sometime.

On reaching home he spoke to his father, "O' Father, how is it you told me that you have instructed me enough, without so doing? If I were instructed well I would not have faced a situation where I could not answer even a single question put to me by the Pānchāla king." He then narrated to his father all that had happened, repeating the questions asked by king Jaivali. Thereupon the oldman said, "O' dear son! Believe me, I, too, do not know the answers to these questions. Had I known so, I would have instructed you on them. Let us both go to king Pravāhaṇa and be instructed on these matters. The boy, who perhaps was embarrassed quite a bit, took leave of his father for not facing the Pānchāla king again. Āruṇi then went to Pānchāla and sought audience of king Pravāhaṇa.

After exchange of usual courtesies Āruṇi Gautama requested the king to instruct him on the issues raised by him (the king) with Śvetketu earlier. Since it was uncommon for a Brāhmin to seek instruction from a Kşātriya, the king had some hesitation. However, on a second thought said he, "O' Gautama, stay over here for a while. As you tell me, this knowledge has not reached the Brāhmins as yet; the instruction on the subject has to be imparted by a Kşātriya only. "Āruṇi Gautama then decided to stay with the king as his student. On an appropriate occasion, the instruction commenced.

(At this stage, it would be worth a while to recall the eight essential components of a Vedic sacrificial fire (yajńa). These eight components are: a designated place for performing the ritual, fuel, smoke, flame, coals, sparks, oblations and finally the reward for performing the ritual.)

Spoke Pravāhaṇa, "There exist five sacrificial fires in the Universe.

"The universe as such is a sacrificial fire place, its fuel is the sun, the rays of the sun are the smoke, the day is its flame, the moon is its coal and the stars are its sparks. The gods offer their faith (śraddhā) as oblations and soma (water in the form of vapours) is their reward."

"The gathering cloud (Parjanya) is the second sacrificial fire place, the air is its fuel, the rain cloud (abhram) is the smoke, lightning is the flame, the thunderbolt is the coal and thundering are the sparks. The sun-rays (deva) offer vapours as oblations and therefrom emerges the rain."

"The earth (pṛthvi) is the third sacrificial fire place, the year (samvatasara) is the fuel, sky is the smoke, the night (rātri) is the flame, the directions (disa) are the coal and the intermediary directions are the sparks. The clouds offer rain as oblations and therefrom is produced the food (anna).

"The male (puruṣa) is the fourth sacrificial fire place, speech (vāk) is the fuel, the life breath (prāṇa) is the smoke, the tongue (jihvā) is the flame, the eyes are the coal and the ears are the sparks. The food is offered as an oblation whereform the semen (retaḣ) is produced."

The female (yoṣā) is the fifth sacrificial fire place, the man's organ is the fuel, the inviting desire is the smoke, the vulva (yoni) is the flame, the sex act inside (anteḣ-karoti) is the coal and the pleasures its sparks. The semen is offered as an oblation whereby the conception (garbha) takes place. Having remained encased for some nine months in the membrane containing water, this foetus takes birth, as ordained."

"This is how" continued Pravāhaṇa "water in the fifth oblation becomes a person. And that O' Gautama is the answer to the fifth question put by me to your son[1]."

"Once the given age expires, the person dies. Then the all-pervading fires carry him to the places wherefrom he had come on taking birth. His body is consigned to fire because it was born out of the oblations given unto the five fires (panchāgni). At this stage the two paths *viz.* the one leading to the world of gods and the other leading to the world of fathers separate. And, that is the answer to the fourth question" Pravāhaṇa said.

Pravāhaṇa further stated "persons who possess knowledge of the said five fires as also persons who having renounced everything and dwelling in the forests meditate on the Lord with faith day and night, on leaving this body take to the path of light. On being consigned to fire they pass on to flame.

"From the radiance of the flame (archi) they successively move on to the bright day (ahaḥ) the fortnight of the waxing moon (śukla-pakṣa), the six months of the year during which the sun moves northwards (uttarāyana), the sun (āditiyam),

---

[1] The nature's process of creation has been perceived here as a continuously performed sacred ritual; both at the cosmological and the physiological planes. In this process the gods and all other elements of nature working in harmony create suitable conditions for the arrival of a new life. The five eternal fires described here are interlinked inseparably wherein the reward of performing a particular sacrifice, becomes an oblation for the next one. In the chain, sun, air and water play pivotal roles.

the moon (chandramā) and the lightning (vidyutam)[2]. Since the merits earned by such persons are limitless they are escorted[3] to the world of Brahma from where they do not return[4]. This is the path of gods (the Devayāna).

"On the other hand, those who live in villages (meaning habitations as opposed to forest dwellers) and perform the prescribed rituals and works, provide succour to other living beings, follow the path of non-injury to others, give alms, undertake charities and lead lives in faith and love, on being consigned to fire pass on to smoke. From the smoke (dhoom- daśā[5]) they successively pass on to night

---

2 The various stations mentioned on the path that a person takes after death *viz.* the flame, the day, the sun, the moon and the like are not the physical bodies or elements as are visible to the human beings. The names indicate the deities identified with each element or heavenly body so mentioned. Such deities carry the jivātmā (the soul-life aggregate) from one station to the other. The expression 'year' denotes fullness.

3 The expression 'escort' has been interpreted variously in the context. The word used is amānavaḥ which means a being who is not human. It also means a being created from the mind of the Hiraṇyagarbha. Āchārya Śankara interprets it in the sense of being immeasurable in merit. Such merits by themselves escort him to Brahmaloka. This is the position taken in this work.

4 In essence this allegory establishes the power and supremacy of faith. The persons who lead their lives truthfully and in faith (satya, śraddhā) keep rising higher and higher staying always in the realms of light. At the end, they merge into the light eternal. The expression 'light' in the context does not mean the optical light but the light of the soul.

5 The various stations on this path, too, viz. smoke, night, moon etc are not the elements as perceived by human senses but the

(rātrim), to the dark- fortnight (kṛṣṇa-pakṣa) and to those six months of the year during which the sun moves southwards (dakṣiṇāyana). However, from these six months they do not pass on to the whole year (samvatsara[6]) but go to the world of fathers. This is the path of the fathers' *viz.* the Pitryāna.

From the world of fathers they move on to space (ākāśām), and from space to moon (Chandramā), where having been offered by gods as oblation as faith in the first of the five sacrificial fires they are established like soma. By this stage is exhausted much of the stock of merits earned by them through deeds and works during life-time. Then taking the residuum of merits with them they move to air, from air to rain via clouds, from rain to food in the form of medicines, vegetation, seeds and pulses, from food to semen, from semen to foetus and thus are they born again. This is how their cycle of births continues. Getting out of this painful process is extremely difficult[7].

There are two categories of beings who take to the path of the fathers. In the first category come those whose conduct had been good. They are rewarded to be born easily and in a worthy life-form (yoni) like that of a learned man or of a warrior or of a trader-farmer-artisan[8]. The other

---

deities identified with these elements etc. These deities take the soul from one station to the other.

6 Meaning thereby that they do not enjoy the full bliss as do those souls which take the path of light.

7 Śankarāchārya in his commentary provides a graphic elucidation of such a difficulty. He recounts innumerable uncertainties about rebirth as a human being. Even when one is so born by dint of the merits of his works, he may not be in a position to break the shackles of life and death. Hence the grind goes on.

8 A fair number of the humans fall in the second category ie amongst those who on death take to the path of the fathers'

beings, whose conduct was unbecoming go to take birth in the despised life-forms such as that of a dog, or of a swine or a lowly human. And this is the answer to the third question. So are O Gautama, the first and the second question answered.

"And yet there are those who take to neither of the aforementioned paths. Theirs is the third case which is called 'be-born (jāyesva), and be-dead (mṛsva)'.

These beings include small creatures. Since even after death these creatures remain in this world only; the world yonder never gets filled up. This third state should be despised. "Thus are answered all the questions." (The

---

viz. the ones whose conduct during their lifetime was good, if not ideal. People generally perform the prescribed rituals and contribute to charities, though not quite understanding the subtleties of Brahma-vidyā or the knowledge of Brahma. The beauty of the allegory lies in the perception of the various stations on the path. For example, on being consigned to fire, such mortals pass on to the state of smoke. The smoke connotes shakiness or unstability as oppose to stability of light. Also, smoke is a mix of light and darkness (prakāśāprakāśā yukta) and not darkness alone. Similarly, a night (rātri) is not altogether darkness. It always possesses some measure of light provided by the moon and the stars. It gives the feeling of repose and rest, too. Assuredly, same thing can be said about the fortnight of the waning moon as also about total darkness. The essence is that those who belong to the world of fathers receive a mixed package of rewards and punishments. Like the smoke rises high only to the extent to which it can be sustained by the heat propelling it upwards and then descends to earth; even so such jivas rise high only to the extent to which they are sustained by the merits of their good deeds. Eventually, descending on earth they are born again and again.

expression despise in the context has been used to arouse hatred for falling into such a situation and to motivate to work our way up for staking claims for the better paths. It should not be construed as derogatory for those jivas who have landed in that situation.)

Pravāhaṇa Jaivali then proceeded to describe such people who commit the five grave sins and fall from the human scale. These sins include stealing of gold, consuming of alcohol, invading of guru's bed, killing of a learned person and keeping company of all such sinners.

The parable concludes with a mention of the rewards awaiting those who meditate on the five sacred fires and conduct their lives in accordance with the prescribed dharma. Such people, it is mentioned, are not affected by sin even if they fall in the company of sinners. Instead, the sinners are converted into saints when they come in contact with such meritorious people.

******

The seer of the parable has perceived that a chain of great sacrificial fires is being performed as a continuum. Commencing at the celestial plane and reaching upto the human plane all that is happening constitutes one part of the divine scheme of creation. Similarly, the Law Divine also lays down specific paths, as the second part of the same scheme, which the beings take on completion of their allotted time on earth so as to collect their rewards in the worlds yonder.

The questions examined by Pravāhaṇa and Āruṇi always have agitated the human mind. Where do we go to after death? Do we ever come back? If so, in what manner do we return? Is it possible to obtain liberation from the cycle of deaths and births? How are the meritorious ones separated from the sinners when the moment of reckoning arrives? Verily, king Jaivali was neither the first nor the last of philosophers to meditate on these issues. All the same, he has left behind a piece of splendid speculative logic which is great in its conception, range and depth. Many other great thinkers of all ages and places also have tried to provide glimpses of the unknown worlds hereafter. Have these riddles been solved to any degree of finality? The answer, of course, is in the negative. Nevertheless, the efforts of such seers have not gone in vain.

The Upaniṣadic belief in this regard may be summarized thus: Firstly, the soul (Ātman) is eternal, attributeless, and beyond rewards and punishments. Once it acquires a body, it however is held in bondage of deaths and births which is full of misery, as it were. Secondly, the perishing and reproduction of species (yonis) are regulated by Divine Law. Thirdly, the human beings enjoy a status of pre-eminence in the creation because of their power to break the barriers of illusion and ignorance (māyā). Consequently, liberation from the cycle of births and deaths is possible during or at the end of this life-form (yoni) alone. Fourthly, those humans who lead lives of piety, charity and austerity move up in the scale while those who lead their lives purely as dictated by senses descend in the scale. To be born as a human being therefore, is a great privilege. It should be taken as an exceptional opportunity for obtaining proximity to the Brahma, the endless and fathomless ocean of truth, consciousness and bliss.

Chhāndogya Upaniṣad
Bṛhadāraṇykopaniṣad

Chapter 9

From The Self Alone Is All Obtained

Sanatkumāra's Instruction to Nārada

Prolegomena

The sages Sanatkumāra and Nārada, the two characters of this parable taken from the Chhāndogyopaniṣad, are well-known personages in the Indian tradition for their piety and wisdom. Although no precise account of their historicity is available, the two have left behind a legacy of timeless appeal. Sanatkumāra literally means the one who is eternally a child. Perhaps, he was the youngest of the four brothers namely Sanata, Sanandana, Sanātana, and Sanatkumāra; who are believed to be the sons of Brahmā and who are alluded to during the daily rituals conducted in accordance with the Paurānic prescription.

It goes without saying that Ṛṣi Sanatkumāra was a person of great learning at some stage of the Indian tradion.

Nārada muni[1] is known equally well in the folklore and philosophic heritage of India. Surprisingly, sage Nārada is nowhere mentioned in the other ancient Upaniṣads. But, at a later stage he acquired a legendary status. Obviously, a dialogue between two of the giant thinkers of their time could not be an ordinary episode. Nārada has two meanings *viz.* the one who provides knowledge about God and one who causes disintegration in a group of people by creating friction.

The Parable

Once, the well-known muni Nārada approached Ṛṣi Sanatkumāra for receiving instruction. The great saint knew that Nārada was not one of the usual students who often approached him with such requests. With a view to deciding upon the course of instruction for him the sage asked the visitor to mention all that he had learnt already.

Replied Nārada, "O' Venerable Sir, I have learnt the Ṛgveda, the Yajurveda, the Sāmaveda and the fourth Ved, the Atharvaveda by heart. Besides, I have learnt the fifth one, *viz.* the history, the Brāhmaṇgrantha (purāṇas), the key to the Vedas viz. the grammar (Vyākaraṇa), the science of propitiation of the fathers (Pitr-śrāddha Vijńāna), the number- science viz. arithmetic (rāśi), the science of portents (daivya vidyā). The chronology and the science of time (nidhi vidyā), logic (tarkaśāstra), the science of polity and ethics (niti śāstra), the science of gods (deva-vidyā), the science of ultimate knowledge (Brahmavidyā) including education, the stages of creation (kalpa), the meter of poetry

---

1 The expression Muni means the one who is absorbed in silent thought.

(chhanda), the science of physical elements (bhuta-vidyā) like zoology (prāṇi vidyā), the science of war making (kşātra-vidyā), astronomy (graha vidyā), the science of serpents (sarp vidyā) and the fine arts like dance, music and architecture (nṛtya-geet vidyā and śilpa). Sir, these entire disciplines do I know".

After a brief pause Narda continues, "O' Venerable Sir, even after acquiring all this knowledge I know only the text and have not yet realized the self because I have heard from the knowers of the truth, like you that the one who has realized the self goes beyond all sorrow. And, here I am in deep sorrow. Kindly help me in crossing over to the other side of the sorrow."

Having heard Nārada providing details of his learning, the great master spoke, "O' Nārada, whatever you have learnt and studied so far is merely the name. All the Vedas, the ancient lore and the branches of science recounted by you were merely the names. Meditate on the name. He, who meditates on name for the purposes of reaching Brahma, obtains freedom of access only to the extent to which the name goes and not beyond that."

Nārada: "O' Venerable one! Is there anything greater than the name? If it is so, kindly educate me about the same."

Sanatkumāra: "O' Nārada, speech (vāk) verily is greater than the name. Through speech alone one comes to know of all the Vedas and other branches of knowledge as have been learnt by you. Through speech alone are known the other disciplines of knowledge like those concerning heaven (Diva-loka) earth, (Pṛthvi) air (Vāyu) Ether (Ākāśā) water (Āpas), light (tejaḥ), botany (Tṛṇ-vanaspati), beasts (Hinsr-Jantu) and worms-flies-ants (akit-patanga-pipeelakam). Through speech alone can one come to know about the right and the wrong as also about truth and falsehood, good and bad and pleasant and unpleasant. Meditate on speech, O' Nārada but remember that one who meditates on speech for the purpose of attaining Brahma obtains freedom to the extent to which speech goes and not beyond that."

Nārada: "O' Venerable Sir, is there anything greater than speech too? If it is so, kindly educate me about the same.

Sanatkumāra: The mind (manas) is superior to speech. The mind holds firm both the name and the speech like a close fist holds two acorns or two berries or two dice-nuts. Only when one makes-up the mind through mind to learn the chants one learns. Only when one makes up the mind through mind to undertake works one performs works. When through mind one desires to have sons and animals, one so desires. Similarly, when one desires for this world and the world beyond, one desires so. Therefore, O' Nārada, mind is superior to speech. The mind is the self (ātmā) because through mind alone is self seen as the doer and receiver of fruits of all works. The mind is the world because through mind alone is the existence of worlds known. The mind is Brahma because through mind alone all efforts to reach Him are made. O' Nārada, meditate on mind. But remember he who meditates on mind for the purpose of attaining Brahma obtains freedom to the extent to which the mind goes and not beyond that."

Nārada: O' Venerable Sir, is there anything higher than mind, too? If so, kindly educate me about the same."

Sanatkumāra: "Resolution (sankalpa) is assuredly higher than mind. Only when one resolves to do, one directs the mind to undertake it. For example, when after due deliberations one resolves to learn certain chants; one inspires the speech through mind to recite the chants in which the name is rooted. The sacred chants abide in the name and the works abide in the sacred chant.

In sum, the pivot of the name, the sacred chants and the sacred works is the will or the resolution. The heaven and earth function as resolved and so do the air and ether. In consequence of their resolution of the rain food becomes willed and from the will of the food the life (prāṇa) becomes willed. From the resolution of the life, the sacred chants are willed and due to their will are the worlds (lokas) willed. Ultimately, from the resolution of the worlds is everything willed. So meditate on resolution, O' Nārada! But remember, he who meditates on resolution with the purpose of attaining Brahma, obtains freedom only to the extent to which the sankalpa goes and not beyond that."

Nārada: "O' Venerable Sir, is there anything greater than the resolution, too? If so, kindly educate me about the same."

Sanakumara: "Consciousness (Chitta) is superior to resolution. When one is conscious about taking something or leaving it one resolves. Thereafter the mind is set in motion to inspire speech for the purpose of speaking the name. The name and the sacred chants then become one and so do the sacred chants and the sacred works. The will or the resolution is rooted in consciousness even when some one knows much but is not conscious of his knowledge, people say he does not know. On the contrary, even if one knows only a little but is conscious of his knowledge people flock to him for learning. Therefore, consciousness is the stay of all these things. The self can be realized only through stable consciousness. Meditate on consciousness O' Nārada! But remember, one who meditates on consciousness for the purpose of attaining Brahma attains freedom only to the extent the consciousness goes and not beyond that."

Nārada; "O' Venerable Sir, is there anything superior to consciousness, too? If so, kindly educate me about the same."

Sanatkumāra: "Concentration (dhyāna) is superior to consciousness. Behold ye! The earth, the ether, the heaven, the waters, the mountains are all stable as if they are in deep concentration. Only through concentration man becomes wise or attains godhood. On the contrary, those who lack concentration create friction among people. They only see the shortcomings of others. When close by, they even describe someone's faults as his strong points but when away they talk ill of them. Such people are assuredly petty. Since they are not aware of what is right or wrong their intellect is never on one focus. But those who are masters of men achieve this station only through concentration. Therefore, O' Nārada meditate on concentration (dhyāna) but remember one who meditates on concentration, his reach remains limited to the extent that concentration goes and not beyond that."

So goes on the inquiry.

Sanatkumara: "(Vijńāna) is superior to concentration.

We come to understand the Vedas and all other departments of knowledge through Vijńāna alone. Assuredly, through Vijńāna Śāstra alone one understands about the truth and falsehood, good and bad, pleasant and unpleasant and this world and the one yonder. Therefore, O' Nārada study the Śāstra concerning Vijńāna[2]. Remember however that he who studies this Śāstra becomes knowledgeable and attains the worlds of knowledge but his reach is limited to the extent to which Vijńāna goes and not beyond."

"Strength (balam) is greater than Vijńāna because one strong person can shake a hundred knowledgeable persons. Since strength enables one to serve one's teacher, he is in a position to listen, see, contemplate and realize the true

---

[2] Vijńāna means the specific understanding of material things.

teachings. Consequently, he becomes the doer and knower. It is all because of strength that earth, ether, the world of light, mountains, noble people, animals, birds, vegetation, beasts and everything else find their stability. O' Nārada meditate on strength[3].

But he who depends on strength to attain Brahma has reach only so far as the strength goes and not beyond."

"Food (Anna) verily is superior to strength. See, if one does not take food for ten days, one will either die or will be as good as dead. Even if he is able to keep his body and soul together, he can neither see things in their right perspective (adrşta) nor can he properly listen (aśrota). Similarly, he is unable to contemplate (amanta) or realize (abodha) or act (akartā) or know things. But once he gets some food to eat he regains all such qualities. Mediate on food, therefore O' Nārada, he who considers food as the means to attain Brahma obtains company of the happy people who have plenty to eat and drink. All the same, he who meditates on food for the purpose of attaining Brahma reaches only to the extent to which the food goes and no length beyond that."

"Water (āpas) alone is superior to food. When there is no rain the food becomes scarce and all living beings turn unhappy. But whenever there is good rain there is happiness all around because then food becomes available in abundance. This earth, the space, the worlds of light, the mountains, all gods and humans, animals, birds, vegetation, beasts, insects and other smaller living beings are all nothing but various forms of water only. Meditate on water O' Nārada, he who meditates on water for the purposes

---

3 Meaning thereby, to understand the nature of strength in all its facets

of attaining Brahma gets all his desires fulfilled and gets freedom of reach to the extent that water goes. Not beyond."

"Tejaħ[4] is greater than water because the former (as heat) is the cause of the latter. Assuredly, heat taking air in company warms up the sky. Then, every one says it is burning hot, it might rain.

"In due course heat produces water. It also causes lightning. Then, the lightning darts forth in all directions and the thundering rain clouds move about or emerge in the sky. Seeing the lightning and hearing the clouds thunder people say, it appears it would rain. Since, heat creates such a scenario; verily it is the producer of water. So Nārada, think ye deeply about heat. He who thinks deeply about the nature of heat as means of attaining Brahma obtains shining glory for himself and worlds unfettered by any darkness. But remember O' Nārada that tejaħ will take you only to the lengths to which it goes and not beyond,

"The space (ākāś) alone is greater than heat (tejaħ). In the space alone are the Sun and the Moon located and so are established lightning, galaxies and the entire thermal energy (Agnaiya Śakti) through space one calls the other, through space one listens to the other and through space alone one answers. In space one actively enjoys or does not enjoy. All are born in the space and all nurture themselves therein (ākāśam-abhijāyate). Since the part is always smaller than the whole, the heat (tejaħ) being a part of the space is of lesser value. So, O' Nārada, meditate on the space. He, who meditates on the space for the purpose of attaining Brahma, attains the worlds of space and light which are the abodes of broad minded people having no pains of mind and body.

---

4 Tejaħ denotes a combination of heat and light.

Besides, he attains freedom of reach to the extent that the space goes, though no more."

"Memory (Smaraṇa) alone is superior to space. For, if some people who have no memory assemble in a place, they will not be able to interact among themselves as they will neither be able to speak, nor listen, nor think nor answer[5].

On the other hand, once in possession of memory[6], they will be able to listen, think and have specific knowledge. It is through memory alone that one knows his sons or the cattlehead. O' Nārada, think you deeply on memory. He, who meditates on the nature of memory as a means of attaining Brahma, attains reach upto the extent that the memory goes, not beyond."

Hope (āśā) alone is superior to memory. Prompted by hope one acquires memory. Having acquired memory one learns the chants and then carries out the sacred works. By hope alone one desires sons and cattleheads, this world and the one yonder[7]. Meditate on hope, O' Nārada he who meditates on hope for the purpose of attaining Brahma obtains fruits of his choicest desires. All his prayers get fulfilled[8]. Besides, he attains freedom of access to the extent that hope goes and not a length beyond."

"The life-breath (prāṇa) alone is higher than hope. As are the spokes of a chariot-wheel fixed onto its hub so are all things fixed onto the life-breath. The life-breath functions

---

5 Obviously, the space shall have no use for them.

6 Internalization of an experience is memory.

7 The basic idea is that hope or motivation is the root of desires and desires set the faculty of memory in motion. Hope or motivation therefore is greater than memory.

8 Obviously, a hopeless person or the one who is left with no motivation can attain nothing, whatever else is to his support.

on its own strength. It gives strength to all others even to itself and for itself. The life-breath is father, mother and brother, sister, the teacher and the Brāhmin[9]. If a person speaks in derogatory terms about his father, mother, brother, sister, teacher or a Brāhmin, people take him to task and call him a slayer of all these venerable ones. But, once the life-breath leaves them, even when he burns them altogether after hitting them by a poker, no one talks ill of him.

"One who knows this truth about the life-breath achieves greater wisdom by seeing things from all possible standpoints and thus becomes an excellent speaker (ativādin[10]). People generally do not like an individual who speaks for the truth fearlessly. They rise against him and create conditions of fear and unpleasantness for him. Under such adverse circumstances, some individuals leave the path of speaking for truth. But, if one is challenged to be a speaker of truth, one should accept being so because hiding of truth results in darkness."

Having heard that the life-breath was greater than everything and that all else was dedicated to it, Nārada did not proceed to ask his usual question as to whether there was something still greater. There could be three possible reasons for his silence *viz.* either he knew that there was nothing greater than the Prāṇa or he felt that one should not put too many questions to a teacher or he was sure that a kind teacher would himself take the instruction to a logical conclusion. In the light of the discourse, it must have become known to Nārada that Brahma is higher than the prāṇa. So, his silence was born of discretion as he knew that the instruction was yet to reach its grand finale.

---

[9] Life is the basis of all relationships.

[10] The one who unhesitatingly speaks in favour of truth

Continued the sage Sanatkumāra, "He, who speaks the truth only is an excellent speaker."

Nārada: "O' Venerable Sir, be kind to me so that I become an excellent speaker of truth".

"Sanatkumāra: "Then, desire to know the truth alone, O' Nārada."

Nārada: "I desire to know the truth."

Sanatkumāra: "Know ye O' Nārada, he who knows and understands the Truth (Brhama) alone can speak the truth. Therefore, desire to know and understand the Truth."

Nārada: "O' Venerable sir, I so desire to know and understand."

Sanatkumāra: "Assuredly, he who contemplates[11] knows. No one can know without contemplation but when one contemplates one knows. O' Nārada, one should desire to contemplate."

Nārada: "O' Venerable One. I desire to know the process of contemplation in specific."

Sanatkumāra: "He who has faith (śraddhā) alone can contemplate. Therefore O' Nārada one should desire to know of faith in specific." (It is quite possible that if one applies one's mind to know the truth without faith, one may land up in the quagmire of contradictions[12].)

Nārada: "O' Venerable Sir, I have the desire to possess faith".

---

[11] The idea is that a person who is contemplative about the true nature of things alone is able to distinguish between the truth and the falsehood and not the one who blindly accepts things as stated. In other words, the 'knowing' by itself is an outcome of 'meditative-thinking' or 'contemplation'. Here the subtle difference between awarenss and knowing is to be seen.

[12] 'Faith must precede knowledge' is an adage.

Sanatkumar: "He who is steadfast (niṣtĥāvāna) alone can have faith[13]. "One who does not possess steadfastness can not achieve faith. So, O' Nārada, have the desire to know of steadfastness in specific."

Nārada: "O, Venerable Sir, I have the desire to obtain the specific knowledge of steadfastness."

Sanatkumāra: "Verily, O' Nārad, only through activity (kṛti) can one achieve steadfastness. One cannot be steadfast in one's faith without involving oneself in the concerned activities[14]. Therefore, desire ye to know specifically about activity."

Nārada: "O' Venerable Sir, I desire to know in specific about activity.'

Sanatkumāra: "Know ye O' Nārad that only when one gains happiness (sukham), one involves oneself in activity. No one wants to do things unless one derives happiness out of such actions. Therefore, happiness alone is worth knowing about."

---

13 Obviously, a wavering mind can never have lasting faith. The source of all conflicts of human beings is the mind or what is now called the psyche. Mind indeed is the hub of the wheel of life with emotions, intellect, attitudes, value system and the like functioning like its spokes. If there is some conflict between the mind and the intellect, between the intellect and the value system or within the multiple layers of mind itself, nay within the layers of intellect per se, these tensions/conflicts shall find manifestation in skewed behavior. Such conflicts are resolved through spiritual wisdom alone.

14 It is explained further that such activities include control of organ of knowledge and action (indriyaṇām-vaśikarnam) and concentration of consciousness (chittaikāgrata).

Nārada: "O' Venerable sir, I possess the desire to know about happiness in particular."

Sanatkumāra: "Listen ye O' Nārad, the Infinite (Bhumā[15]) alone is happiness. The small (alpa[16]) has no happiness to offer. So, the Infinite alone is worthy to be desired."

Nārada: "O' Venerable Sir, I desire to know the Infinite. Do kindly instruct me on the Infinite."

Sanatkumāra: "When one sees nothing else, listens nothing else and knows nothing else that is the Infinite. But where one sees something else, listens something else and knows something else that is finite. Assuredly, the Infinite is immortal (amṛtam) while the finite is liable to decay i.e mortal (mṛtyam).

Nārada: "Please tell me on what is the Infinite established?"

Sanatkumāra: "On its own greatness (Sve-mahimni) or assuredly not on its own greatness either. In this world people set possession of cows, horses, elephants, camels, servants, fields and dwellings as the norms of greatness. When I refer to greatness in the context of the Infinite I do not mean all these things because all such things are established on other things[17]. I now give you a discourse on the greatness as pertains to the Infinite."

"That alone is below. That alone is above. That alone is the west or behind (paśchim) and that alone is to east or in front (purva). That alone is the north as also to the south. Verily, that alone is established in this entire universe. This is how the omnipresence of the Infinite is stated in the

---

15 The expression Bhumā has been used to denote the completeness of Brahma. It means greater than everything else.

16 The expression 'alpa' signifies the finite; small in all respects.

17 The Infinite could not be established on something else.

third person. The same can be stated in the first person (ahamakārādeśa) as follows[18]. I alone am above. I alone am below. I alone am behind. I alone am in front. I alone am to the north. I alone am to the south. Verily, I alone am established in the entire universe."

"Now listen ye the same in terms of self (ātamādeśa) 'The self alone is above. The self alone is below. The self alone is behind. The self alone is in front. The self alone is to the north. The self alone is to the south. Verily, the self alone is established in the entire universe."

"The wiseman who seeing, thinking and knowing thus finds delight in the Infinite Self (Ātmarati[19]) has pleasure in the Infinite Self (Ātmakṛda) obtains union with the Infinite Self (Ātma mithuna) and enjoys the bliss in the Infinite Self, alone is the master of himself (svarāj that is self ruler). He the wise man has unfettered access to all worlds. But those who believe otherwise than this are ruled by others (anyarājam). They belong to the world of mortals and possess no freedom of access to other worlds."

Summing up the discourse, the sage proceeded, "Assuredly, the wise man who thus sees, thinks and knows the Infinite in reality obtains the life breath (prāṇa) from the Self, hope (āśā) from the Self, memory (smṛti) from the Self, space (ākāś) from the Self, heat (tejaḥ) from the Self, water (jalam) from the Self, the feelings of light and darkness (avirbhāvtirobhāva) from the Self, food (annam) from the Self, strength (balam) from the Self, knowledge in specific (Vijńāna) from the Self, mind (manas) from the Self, speech (vāk) from the Self, the name from the Self, the

---

[18] Ahamakārādeśa, means as has been instructed by the Infinite

[19] Deriving pleasure from internal experience

chant (mantra) from the Self, the sacred works from the Self, indeed from the Self itself is obtained everything."

"That seer of the Infinite (Brahmadarśi) sees neither death, nor disease nor distress. He sees the Infinite alone. Eventually, since he obtains the All-pervasive he obtains everything[20].

This is how by expanding the true knowledge the great sage Sanatkumāra showed the path of light to Nārada so as to enable him to negotiate through the darkness of ignorance.

*****

Besides its immense philosophical value, the conceptual beauty of the parable lies in the fact that the great teacher Sanatkumāra leads his student onto the path of light proceedings from the known to the unknown and from the gross to the subtle refining the seeker's perceptions shade by shade and building up his premises on the sound foundations of rationality.

Chhāndogyopaniṣad

---

[20] The idea is that the one who desires to realize the self through self alone acquires the capacity to do what he wills. Once one knows the self (the finite) the knowing of the Self (the Infinite) becomes obvious.

Chapter 10

In the Self Alone Are All Names And Forms Established

Instruction to Indra-Virochana

Prolegomena

The names of Indra and Virochana, the main characters of this story, often appear in the Vedic literature. Who were they? During the ancient times, the people who conducted their lives as per the tenets of the Vedic faith were known as devas while the others were called asuras. Indra was the king of devas and Virochana was the king of asuras. It seems, initially these expressions denoted the designations of the high public offices of these personages. Later, with the spread of the Vedic civilization, Indra gained ascendancy in public esteem over his rival, Virochana. Also, the terms deva and asura became respectively synonymous of gods and demons. Etymologically, while Indra means the possessor of bounties, Virochana means the one who possessed special lights. In this story the two appear to be equals with Indra enjoying some edge over his rival. Their common preceptor is Prajāpati, the Creator, and father of all.

The Parable

Once, at some place during a sermon Prajāpati had said, "That Supreme Being, who is untouched by sin and is unaffected by age, who is beyond the reach of death and sadness and is unaffected by hunger and thirst and who is true in action and resolve alone should be sought for and that he who seeks Him alone for self purification and self-liberation obtains fulfillment of his desires and access to all the worlds."

When the message of Prajāpati's sermon reached Indra and Virochana, they called the assemblies of their respective people and obtained their permission for seeking knowledge of the Supreme Being and thereby get access to all the worlds and fulfillment of all desires. Having so resolved, they approached Prajāpati with fuel for the sacrificial fire (fire-wood) in their hands[1]. Once the initial formalities were over, they were admitted to the hermitage (āśrama) where they stayed for thirty two years receiving instruction along with other students. At the conclusion of the course of study, when the other students departed from the hermitage Indra and Virochana stayed back. Prajāpati had known that they were not satisfied with the instruction imparted to them during the normal course. He, therefore, asked them, "Say, what brings you to me?"

Replied they, "O' Venerable Sir, the knowledgeable people speak of a discourse with regard to the Supreme Being who is the bestower of all worlds and all desires. Both

---

[1] This was the standard practice during the period. All seekers of knowledge approached their teachers with fuel in their hands.

of us have stayed over here to know about that Supreme Being[2]."

Spoke the Prajāpati, "The one whom you see in the eye (akṣi)[3]. This is immortal (amṛt), this is without fear (abhaya) and this is great (Brahma).

They asked, "O' Venerable one! Who is the self whom we see in the water or in the mirror? Pray, tell us who that self is?"

"He is the one (about whom you are keen to know) whom you see in all these". Saying so the master continued, "O' dear students Indra and Virochana, go and see that self in a vessel full of water. In case you are unable to see him there, do come and ask me."

Both of them looked into a vessel full of clean water.

"What do you find?' asked the Prajāpati.

"We see the self absolutely similar to the two of us from head to feat." Spoke Indra and Virochana.

"Go ye O' Indra-Virochana, clean yourselves well, put on nice clothes and jewellery and then look for the self into the vessel full of water." Said the Prajāpati?

They did as were directed. Again the great teacher asked, "What do you see, now?"

They replied, "O' Venerable One! The two reflected selves that we see are just as well bejewelled, nicely attired and neat and clean in looks as are two of us."

---

2 The point to note here is that there was no basic difference in the characters of Indra and Virochana and as a corollary between devas and the asuras. Both were equally keen to acquire similar knowledge for similar purposes.

3 The word 'akṣi' has two meanings viz. an eye and nature. The understanding of the instruction depended on the particular meaning one chose to apply.

Spoke the Prajāpati, "This is the self."

Hearing this, both of them left the āśrama with their hearts at peace.

Seeing them go thus, Prajāpati mused aloud, "Both of them go without obtaining the true knowledge of the self (the jivātmā and the paramātmā). Therefore, devas and asuras adopting this knowledge would not succeed in their missions."

With peace returning to his heart Virochana went straight to the asuras. His understanding of the instruction of the Prajāpati was that there was no distinction between the self and the body. He told his followers, "In this world body alone is worth worshipping and worthy of all service rendered unto it."

That is why even today to the knowledgeable people all such persons are asuras who offer no alms; possess no faith and who do not perform yajńas. They do so because that is what their (of the asuras'), belief is. They offer food, clothes and jewellery to the dead body in the belief that by doing so they would conquer even the next world.

The matter with Indra was, however, different. On his way back to home, he saw something odd in his understanding of the instruction. Thought he, "Just as by bejewelling this body this reflected self (Chhāyā-Puruṣa) becomes bejewelled and by putting on nice clothes, this reflected self become well-attired, so would it become blind should the body lose the eyes. Similarly, this reflected self would lose an eye or would be torn asunder should the body lose an eye or be torn asunder. And, verily, this self would die in case this body dies. In that case I do not find in it the Being whom I desire to seek."

Since doubt had arisen in his mind, he felt he was not quite capable of imparting true instruction to his fellow devas. So, he returned to Prajāpati with fuel in his hands.

On seeing him so returned, the teacher asked, "O' Indra, you had gone along with Virochan with your heart at peace. What brings you back now?" Indra humbly put forth his doubts as to why he was unable to accept the mere reflection of the body as self.

"You are right 'O' Indra. This self is just as you have thought of it to be. I shall further elaborate on it. But for that you stay here for the next thirty two years." The additional thirty two years, too, passed.

Then Prajāpati spoke to Indra, "It is the same self which joyfully wanders in a dream."

With his earlier doubts having been resolved, peace returned to Indra's heart. He took leave of his teacher and left for his home. Enroute he pondered, "True, even if the body was blind, the self could see things during dream or even if the body had only one eye, the self could move around during dream with both the eyes. During a dream the self does not suffer from the weakness of the body. The self-in-dream (svapnātmā) is not killed or tortured if the body be killed or tortured.[Then a doubt flashed across his mind.] But, the self-in-dream certainly feels as if being chased. It is seen as unhappy and sad. So, this self, too, could not be the one that I seek."

Once again the king of devas returned to Prajāpati's āśrama with the sacrificial fuel in his hands and narrated his doubts to his teacher. Once Indra went through a further stay of thirty two years at the hermitage, instructed Prajāpati, "The self having gone to the state of deep sleep does not see dreams. In this state established in its own self, it enjoys in its own bliss." Satisfied with the new instruction, Indra left for his home. Enroute he mused, 'Verity, this self-in-deep sleep (susuptātmā) does not know distinctly that 'This I am.' Nor does it know other people. So it is as good as dead. Here, too, I do not find the self whom I had desired to seek.

Thinking thus, with sacrificial fuel in his hands he returned to his teacher once again.

On listening to the fresh doubts of Indra, the preceptor said, "O' Indra you are right. The self is exactly the same. I shall further elaborate upon it, but, for that you will have to stay for five more years.

Thus, all told Indra stayed at the hermitage of the Prajāpati for a period of one hundred and one years. The Prajāpati, then, concluded the instruction. "O' Indra, this body, verily, is subject to the regimen of death and is, therefore, perishable. It can never be immortal. It only serves as a place of rest and enjoyment (adhiṣtĥānam) for the self (jivātmā). For this reason alone, so long as the self remains embodied, it partakes all enjoyments and pains. So long as the self remains within the confines of this body it remains attached to all pleasures and pains. But, once it casts off the shackles of this mortal body, the self moves beyond all pleasures and pains[4]."

"Just as the air, the cloud, the lightening and the thunder, all without a body, emerge from sky and having come in contact with the great causal light and remaining established in their respective forms (svain-rupain) merged in the sky, so does the self (jivātmā) while established in its own form [when not embodied] it merges into the Self (the Infinite). Having reached that great ocean of bliss, the self (jivātmā) enjoys fulfillment of all desires through resolution (sankalpa) alone not needing the body for the purpose. In that state, the jiva (prāṇa or the life-breath) remains attached

---

4 It may be noted that pleasures and pains referred to here are the resultant feelings attached to human actions and not to the inherent bliss which is integral to the Self.

to the body just as a horse or a bull remains attached to a chariot[5].

---

[5] Interestingly, on the face of it the instruction contained in the parable suggests duality (dvait) though the Upaniṣads teach non-duality (advait, monism). It appears from the instruction imparted to Indra by Prajāpati that although on liberation from the body the jivātmā merges with the Infinite self, it all the same retains its individual form for purposes of fulfillment of desires. On the other hand, the monistic philosophy of Vedānta posits that on liberation the merger of the infinitesimal self with the Infinite Self is total. There remains thereafter no place for an individual form, desires or their fulfillment whatsoever. Assuredly, the advait philosophy establishes that there is no distinction between the self and the Self and that the perceived distinction between the Inner controller (Antaryāmin) and the outer controller (Bahiryāmin) is all due to non-knowledge (avidyā or māyā). In this context the idea contained in the expression 'in its own form' (svain- rupain) is somewhat perplexing. Such divergent references or seemingly divergent expressions perhaps gave occasion to divergent interpretations and consequent prolificity of faiths.

Śankarāchārya comments:

'All pleasures emanating from fulfillment of desires through pure and noble resolutions (śuddsattva sankalpa) are related to God (Iśwara). The Supreme Being (Pramātmā) alone is the enjoyer of all those pleasures through all his noble limitations (sattva māyā upādhi). Therefore, the Supreme Being alone is the refuge of all the actions born out of non-knowledge ((avidyā-janeya). There is no second. The expression 'established in its own form' is explained thus: 'Rising above this body and forsaking the feeling of body- soul aggregate the self gets established in its own inherent form (satsva-rupa). All it means is that it merges in the Self. So, there is no duality.'

During the waking state the one who is seen inside the eye is the Being who dwells in the eye (chakşus puruşa). The organ of the eye is the medium for him to obtain a view of forms. The one who knows that I smell is the self and the organ of nose is the medium for him to obtain smell. The one who knows that I speak this is the self and the organ of speech is the medium for him to speak words. The one who knows that I contemplate this is the self and the mind (manas) is his divine or supra-natural eye (daivachakşu)[6]. And this self on reaching the state of all pervading Self (sarvātmabhāva) becomes pure and lord of all. Then, assuming the limitation of mind, it sees and enjoys all pleasures through this mind which is the lord of all other senses. This self then sees and enjoys all the pleasures of Brahmalok through resolution alone."

Since Indra received this instruction about the self from Prajāpati (and futher disseminated it to the gods) all gods meditate upon the self. As a fruit of such meditation they have gained access to all pleasures and all worlds. Access to all pleasures and all worlds is obtained by him who like Indra comes to know the self and realizes it following the teaching contained in the scriptures and the instruction imparted by one's preceptor. This is the instruction about self as imparted by Prajāpati for the benefit of all beings[7].

---

6 Since the senses know only of the present (Vartmānkāl-vişayaka) they are not supra- natural. On the other hand, the mind can obtain knowledge of the past, present and future. Also, it can know of the minute and the subtle. It is therefore called the supra-natural eye or the divine eye of the self.

7 The message is that the knowledge of the self (ātam jńāna) and the fruits of such knowledge are the same for all beings and not for the gods alone as may be inferred incorrectly from the context.

***

The message of the instruction is that the Self alone is the sustainer (Nirvāhitā) of all names and forms. Where, all the names and forms are established that is Barhma. The Brahma is immortality (amṛtam) and Brahma alone is the all pervading soul of the Universe.

Chhāndogyopaniṣad.

Chapter 11

The Conditioned and the Unconditioned Brahma

The Parable of Ajātśatru *and Gārgeya*

Prolegomena

This parable is contained in the first chapter of Part Two of the Bṛhadāraṇykopaniṣad. The Upaniṣads say "He who had known the self had known that he was the Self itself[1]," meaning thereby that Ātmā or the non-dual self alone is the subject of knowledge and all other distinctions arise from ignorance. At the cosmic plane the Self manifests in a great variety of phenomena in which the sun, the moon the space and the like form His organs. All these phenomena have their specified roles in the human body too as presiding deities of various senses like the speech, hearing and smell through which the self enjoys to be the conscious doer (kartā) and experiencer (bhoktā), as it were. Witnessed this way, the self is perceived as the Saguṇa Brahma or the

---

[1] Ātmanameyva vedaham Brahmāsmi.

Conditioned Self (Self Attributed). All this is due to avidyā or ignorance. Once avidyā is removed through vidyā (true knowledge) the self retains no name or form. It then is known as the Nirguṇa Brahma or the Unconditioned Self. The Self Attributeless alone is truth and is the subject of knowledge.

The self is the individual soul which in association with ignorance (māyā) appears as jiva i.e. the living being. The jiva is the master and the life breath (prāṇa) is the subordinate. The Supreme Reality (Ātman) limited by the upādhi of the buddhi (intelligence) appears as the jiva.

The parable highlights the truth with regard to the Unconditioned Brahma in an easy to understand way. The characters of the parable seemingly take opposite views, though in reality their stands are complementary. Bālāki Gārgeya a Brāhmin is well-versed in the scared lore pertaining to the Saguṇa Brahma where as the king Ajātśatru is a Kṣatriya who is a knower of the Nirguṇa Brahma. Many a great thinker visited his court to discuss with him subtle issues of philosophy. The meeting between Gārgeya and the ruler of Kāśi had a philosophical significance. The king's ambition was to excel his neighboring king Janaka as a patron of learned people and as a liberal giver of alms.

One day, Dṛpta Bālāki a descendent of the family of ṛṣi Garga, came to meet the king. Perhaps, his purpose was either to make mark as a scholar at the Kāśi court or to earn a handsome reward from the generous king. The visitor proposed to instruct his host on Brahma. The latter readily accepted the proposal

The method of exposition adopted in this parable was quite popular during the Vedic times. In this technique, at the out-set a seemingly unquestionable preposition is put forward by the expositor. Then, the other participant raises a valid question making as if the proposition was only partly true. In doing so, the formulation in question was neither condemned nor was it accepted. The proposer was, thus, impelled to either refine or to altogether revise his hypothesis. This process of making re-statements and raising questions continues until the entire field concerning the issue is analyzed thread-bare. Generally, the discourse proceeds from the known to the unknown and from the gross to the subtle.

The Parable

Once Dṛpta Bālāki of the family of Garga went to Ajātśatru the king of Kāśi and said, "I shall instruct you on Brahma". The king was mighty pleased with the proposition and gave one thousand cows to Gārgeya for the offer. Then the instruction commenced.

Gārgeya," That being (puruṣa) up there in the sun (āditya) is the one upon whom I meditate as Brahma [The being which is identified with the sun and the eye, on entering the body resides in the heart as ego; the doer and the experiencer]. Him do I understand as Brahma and meditate upon as the Being (āditya puruṣa).

Ajātśatru: "No, no. Please do not tell me about that. I worship him as all surpassing (atiṣtĥa-servesām), as the head of all beings and as the rediant one. He who meditates upon him becomes all surpassing, head of all beings and radiant." [That is to say, he (the king) should be told some other aspect or attribute of the Brahma.]

Gārgeya," The being up there in the moon (Chandra), I meditate upon him as Brahma."[The being that resides in the moon as doer and the experiencer (Chandrapuruṣa).]

Ajātśatru: "No, no. Please do not tell me about that. I worship him as the great white-robed radient Soma. He who thus meditates upon him gets abundant soma for his sacrifies and his food never runs short."

Gārgeya," The being up there in the lightning (Vidyut), I meditate upon him as Brahma." [The being that resides in lightening also dwells in the skin and the heart as doer and the experiencer (Vidyutpuruṣa).]

Ajātśatru: "No, no Please do not tell me about that. I worship him as an embodiment of radiance (tejaħvi) He who thus meditates upon him becomes radiant himself and begets radiant offsprings."

Gārgeya: "The being in the ether (ākāśm), I meditate upon him as Brahma [the being that dwells in the ether also resides in the space in heart (hṛdayākāśa) as doer and experiencer (Ākāśa-Puruṣa).]

Ajātśatru: "No, no. Please do not tell me about that. I worship him as the full (purṇa) and the unmoving. He who thus meditates upon him is filled with offsprings and cattlewealth and his offsprings never depart from this world."

Gārgeya: "The being in the air (Vāyu) I meditate upon him as Brahma. [The being that dwells in the air also dwells in the life-breath (prāṇa) and the heart as doer and the experiencer (Vāyu-puruṣa)].

Ajātśatru: "No, no. Please do not tell me about that. I worship him as the Lord, the irresistible and as the unvanquished army. [The group of gods classified as Maruts are always taken as an army]. He who thus worships him becomes victorious, unconquerable and a defeater of his enemies."

Gārgeya: "The being in the fire (Agni), I meditate upon as Brahma. [The being that resides in fire also resides in the speech (vāk) and in the heart as doer and experiencer (Agni-puruṣa)]".

Ajātśatru: "No, no. Please do not tell me about that. I worship him as forbearing. He who thus worships him becomes forbearing and begets forbearing offsprings."

Gārgeya: "The being in the water (āpaḥ), I meditate upon as Brahma. [The being that dwells in water also dwells in the semen and the heart as doer, and experiencer (Āpas-puruṣa)].

Ajātśatru: "No, no. Please do not tell me about that. I worship him as the likeness (pratiroopa). He who meditates upon him thus always gets what is like him or is in his own image and never what is not in his own image. He also gets sons in his own image."

Gārgeya: "The being there in the mirror, I meditate upon as Brahma. [The being that resides in the mirror also resides in other shining objects like swords and in the intellect as doer and experiencer (Adarśa-puruṣa)].

Ajātśatru: "No, no. Please do not tell me about that. I worship him as the shining one. He who worships him thus, verily becomes the shining one. He out- shines those in whose contact he comes. He also gets shining offsprings."

Gārgeya: "The sound that arises behind the one who walks (paśch- śabda) is the Brahma I meditate on" (paśch-śabda puruṣa).

Ajātśatru: "No, no. Please do not tell me about that. I worship him as life. He who meditates upon it thus enjoys the full life span permitted to him according to his previous works. The life does not depart from him during his allotted time for reasons as sickness and the like."

Gārgeya: "The being there in the quarters (diksu), I meditate upon as Brahma [The being that dwells in the quarters also dwells in the two ears and the heart as doer and experiencer]. The reference is to the twin gods Aśvins. They never separate from each other, nor do the quarters from each other (dik-puruṣa).

Ajātśatru: "No, no. Please do not tell me about that. I worship him as an inseparable second. He who meditates upon it thus gets companions and followers who never part company with him.

Gārgeya: "The being out there in the shadow (chhāyā) I meditate upon as Brahma. [The being that resides in the shadow also resides in the external darkness, ignorance and in the heart (chhāyā-puruṣa)].

Ajātśatru: "No, no. Please do not talk to me about that, I worship him as death. He who worships him thus attains a full term of life in this world. Death never approaches him before time."

Gārgeya: "The being, which is here in the self, I worship him as Brahma." [The being in the self resides in the intellect and the heart (Ātma-puruṣa)].

Ajātśatru: "No, no. Please do not tell me about that I worship him as 'Self possessed" (Ātmavān). He who worships him thus himself becomes self-possessed and begets self possessed offsprings."

Since Ajātśatru could provide an elaborate and rational exposition of all that Gārgeya had to offer to him, the latter was left with no more propositions to offer. He, therefore, became silent with shame.

Ajātśatru asked, "Is that all?"

Gārgeya: "Yes, that is all."

Ajātśatru: "But this does not make the Brahma known." (Meaning thereby that why had Gārgeya claimed that he knew about Brahma and could instruct Ajātśatru on that.)

Accepting the fact that Ajātśatru knew more and better than him, Gārgeya requested the king to take him (Gārgeya) as his disciple and instruct him further on Brahma. The king being a Kṣtriya hesitated to assume the role of a preceptor to a Brāhmin as it was against the tradition. Nevertheless, he agreed to provide an exposition of the Reality to Dṛpta Bālāki.

The discourse had proceeded progressively from the gross to the subtle. Starting from the sun Gārgeya had finally reached the self, the ultimate in the Upaniṣadic speculation. Thereafter, nothing else remained to be probed. When Ajātśatru asked the question 'Is that all', Gārgeya could justifiably retort, "What else!" But that was not to be because even the being in the self ie in the ātma puruṣa refers to the one with an attribute of being self-possessed and hence a name and form created by avidyā. The seer of the parable wanted to move from the conditioned self on to the Unconditioned Self. Obviously, the knowledge of the conditioned self is inescapable for perceiving the Unconditioned Self.

The parable proceeds further.

Holding Gārgeya by hand, Ajātśatru took him to a person who was sleeping. The king addressed the sleeping person aloud thus, "O' Great white-robed Soma, the Radiant![2]" The man did not react. But when Ajātśatru pushed him with his hand, the man got up.

The king asked the question, ":O' Gārgeya, This person, who accompanies intelligence or consciousness, when fell asleep where was it (refers to consciousness)? And where did it come back from later?

(Indeed there was only one question which pertained to the position of consciousness; the latter part was superfluous since a person could return only from a place where he

---

2 This is one of the epithets of prāṇa or the life breath

had retreated to.) When Gārgeya could provide no answer, Ajātśatru explained thus:

When this being which is full of consciousness (Vijńāna maya) is asleep, it absorbs for that time all the senses to perceive their respective objects through its own consciousness and rests in space within the heart. When this being takes in these senses it is said to be asleep (svapiti). During this state the abilities to smell, speak, see as also the powers of mind are all absorbed. During the state of deep sleep the ātman forsakes the limitations super imposed by avidyā or māyā and dwells in its natural and absolute self. But, even during this situation the soul does not experience full liberation as it remains covered by a film of ignorance. That is the mystery of the deep-sleep state.

"When this being moves about in dreams, these are the worlds related to his past actions. Then he becomes, as it were, a great king or a great Brāhmin, as it were or attains high and low states, as it were. Like a great sovereign taking with him a body of his people moves about in his country as he pleases, so does the self taking with it the senses (prāṇas) moves about (in his body) as it pleases."

Amplifying the difference between the states of deep-sleep and dreaming, the learned sovereign propounded, "Again, when one goes into deep-sleep (one is aware of nothing whatsoever in this state) one spreads out in all the seventy-two thousand channels called hitās which extend from the heart throughout the body and thus resides in the whole body in the company of consciousness[3]. As a baby or an emperor or a noble Brāhmin lives when he has reached the epitome of bliss, so does one then rest."

---

3 The heart is believed to be the place of residence of intellect i.e buddhi or antahkaraṇa.

That was the reply to the question 'where was it during the deep sleep?' This followed the reply to the second question viz. 'whence did it come back from on being shaken up?'

"As the spider moves up the thread produced by itself, or as the tiny sparks fly off the fire in all directions, so from the self come forth all breaths, all worlds, all divinities and all beings in varied forms. The secret name of the self (the Upanişad) is 'the truth of truth'. The vital breaths are the truth and their truth is the self (the ātman)."

The Teaching[4]

"This individual self, which is of the same nature as is the Supreme Self, being separated from It like a spark of fire, has penetrated the wilderness of the body, the organ etc and although really transcendental, has taken on the attributes of the latter, which are relative and thinks that it is this aggregate of the body and organ, that it is lean or stout, happy or miserable, for it does not know that it is the Supreme Self. But, when a teacher enlightens it, saying that it is not the body etc but the transcendental Supreme Brahma. It then gives up the pursuit of worldly desires and is convinced that it is the Brahma ..."

Bŗhadāraņykopanişad.

---

4 Śankrāchāraya's commentary, Chapter 2, Brāhmaņ (Translation by Swami Nikhilānanda, The Upanişads, Phoenix House Ltd., London, 1957, p.164)

Chapter 12

Thou That Are: Tattwamasi

Uddālaka Āruṇi's Instruction to Śvetketu

Prolegomena

Once again Śvetketu Āruṇeya is the hero of our story and his father Uddālaka becomes his preceptor. The sermon embodied in this parable is one of the masterpieces of abstract philosophy wherein a profoundly subtle subject has been dealt with in a refreshingly easy style.

The family of the sage Aruṇa was known for its tradition in learning and piety. So, when young Śvetketu came of age his father, Uddālaka, wanted him to uphold the high standards of the family in true scholarship and not to remain merely a poor cousin of the Brāhmins[1].

---

[1] The expression used is 'Brahma bandhu' which is a derogatory term used for a person who although born in a Brāhmin family but for lack of learning, over- bearing nature and poor deeds could not be called a Brāhmin.

Therefore, the lad was sent to a hermitage to complete his education and for learning the Vedas. The boy spent as many as twelve years in learning the religious lore and returned home when he was twenty four. Alas! Soon after, the father noticed that in the education of his son there remained much to be desired. To his father's disgust the youngman had developed an overbearing attitude and forsaking the sense of humility had assumed the airs of being a knower of the essence of the Vedas[2] (Veda-tattva-vetā). The father, therefore, decided to proceed with the further education of his son under his personal care.

The Parable

One day, the sage Uddālaka called over his self-conceited son, Śvetketu, and told him that he was anguished to find that certain angularities had developed in his character and that his education was incomplete. With a view to making his son realize his deficiencies, Uddālaka asked him whether he had received that particular instruction by which the unhearable becomes heard (aśrutam śrutam bhavati), the un-perceivable becomes perceived (amatam matam bhavati) and the unknowable becomes knowable (avijyńatam vijyńatam bhavati). Assuming as if he knew all that was worthy of knowing, Śvetketu replied, "O' Venerable Sir, how could that be possible?"[3].

Finding the iron hot, the great ṛṣi decided to strike. In the bargain, Uddālaka unfolded for all times to come some of the most sublime and seminal thoughts of the Vedic knowledge. Uddālaka commenced his discourse thus:

---

2 That is to say, instead of becoming a superior thinker (mahā-manasvi) he had developed a superiority complex (mahā-manā).

3 That is to say, such learning was not possible.

"O' Dear son, just as from a clod of clay one comes to know about all that is made of clay. The clay alone is the truth. The rest are mere names. And what is a name after all? It, verily, is only a form of variety introduced by speech.

"O' Dear son, just as from a nugget of gold, one comes to know all about that is made of gold. The gold alone is the truth. The rest are mere names. And, what is a name after all? It verily, is only a form of variety introduced by speech.

"O' Dear son, just as from an iron piece one comes to know all that is made of iron. The iron alone is the truth. The rest are mere names. And, what is a name after all? It, verily, is only a form of variety introduced by speech. And that is the instruction[4]."

---

4 That is to say: a large variety of objects possessing different shapes, sizes, weights, appearance, utility and many more dimensions are made of clay. Though all such objects are identified with different names, they all possess the same properties as does the clod of clay, which is their substratum. Similarly, all the objects made of gold irrespective of their variegated dimensions possess the essence and qualities of the gold nugget from which these objects are fabricated. The same kind of relationship exists between a piece of iron and all the objects made out of it. Therefore, it comes to pass that in essence the whole, viz. the clod of clay or the nugget of gold or the iron piece, is the same as are its parts, the objects made out of them. So, it is logical to aver that if the part is comprehended in all its dimensions, then the whole, too, is comprehended and that the two viz. the parts and the whole essentially are one. Once this logic is applied to comprehend, so to say, the relationship between the self (the infinitesimal soul) and the Self (the Infinite soul) it becomes evident that the two indeed are one and the perceived difference is created by the variety introduced by speech.

Having said this much the sage paused for a while. The silence however was broken by Śvetketu who in all humility said, "O' Venerable Sir, if such an instruction was known to my respectable teacher, he surely would have imparted the same to me. I pray, you teach me on the subject."

Replied Uddālaka Āruṇi, "So be it".

"Before the creation, there was Being (sat) alone without a second. Some say before the creation there was Non- Being (asat) alone without a second and from that Non-Being the Being emerged. But, how could that viz. emerging of the Being from the Non-Being be possible? So, assuredly, my son, in the beginning there was Being alone, without a second.

"The Being resolved, 'I be many[5]. Let me create[6].' Then, It (sat) created energy (tejas, which is a combination of heat and luminescence). That energy resolved, 'I be many. Let me create.' It (tejaḥ) created water (āpaḥ.)[7]. That water resolved, 'I be many. Let me create.' It (āpaḥ) created food. So where ever there is water there is abundant food. From water only are all foods[8] and eatables produced.

"Corresponding to these three fundamental elements viz. energy, water and earth there are three ways in which species are born. They are either egg-born (andaj) or body born (pindaj) or the sprout-born (Udbhijja) viz. the one

---

5 The expression used, 'bahusyam' which may also mean, 'I am omnipotent.'

6 The expression used, 'prajayeya' which may also mean, 'Let me be born.

7 This is why whenever a living being is subjected to heat water is emitted in the form of perspiration

8 The expression used is "annaḥ' which may also mean earth (pṛthvi) because food is produced from earth and water is its cause.

which springs up after breaking the earth like the plants and other vegetation.

"Then the Supreme Being resolved to enter into the three elements viz. the tejaḥ, the āpaḥ and the pṛthvi along with the life (jivātmā) so as to create and propagate their (of the elements) innumerable forms and names through the triple- permutation combination process. Seen thus, it becomes evident that He alone has given names and forms to all things which contain the essences of each of the fundamental elements in some measure. This science, O' Dear Son, you learn from me clearly.

[Creation or genesis has been an integral part of philosophical speculation always and everywhere. The Upaniṣadic thinkers provided rational foundations to this extremely remote and subtle issue of start point. They attribute it to the resolve (sankalpa) of the Being (the Sat) that 'Let Me Create'. The modern day cosmologists theorize that the universe came into being due to a 'Big Bang' some 14 billion years ago.

Following the dictum 'whatever has had a beginning shall have an end', the Vedic seers speculated upon the reverse of the Creation viz. the Dissolution (parlaya), when all existence shall subsume into the Being for ions to come. Thus, they drew a fine distinction between the perishable creation and the Imperishable Creator. The cosmologists, too, have proffered a corresponding theory of 'the Big Crunch'. They propound that billion of years hence the gravitational forces will begin pulling all and sundry back into the singularity that all was born of. Thus, the Vedic seers were aware of 'energy' being the first manifestation of the Being. The God Particle!

[See, how smoothly yet profoundly does a sage-father impart such a profound knowledge to his loving and worthy inheritor!]

"The redness in the fire (fire being an object produced through the triple[9] permutation-combination process referred to above) is from the tejaħ element, the whiteness from the water element and the blackness from the pŗthvi element. Once you understand it so, the fire loses its distinctive identity viz. the fireness (agnitva) and remains so merely in speech. Therefore, the three elements alone are the reality (satyam).

"The redness in the moon (a form emerged from the triple permutation-combination process) is from the tejas element, the whiteness from the water element and the blackness from the pŗthvi element. Once you understand it so, the moon loses its distinctive identity viz. the moonness (chandratvam) because it is not way different from the three fundamental elements. The differences then remain in name only. And, name verily is no reality. The three elements alone are so (that is to say satyam).

"The red part in the lightning (a form created by the triple permutation-combination process) is that of heat the white part in it is that of water and the black part in it is that of earth. O' dear son, once it is understood so, the lightning loses its distinctive identity viz. the lightningness (vidyuttva) and remains so merely in speech. Therefore, the three elements alone are the reality (satyam).

"The great seers of ancient times who had come to know of this science as revealed through the aforementioned parables always said that no one could ever tell them

---

9 The process denotes a continuous and progressive division of the three elements in a cyclic order and their simultaneous mixing at each division in such a way that the emergent mix each time inherites the essence of the fundamental elements in a certain proportion.

something which they had not heard, perceived or known. To them, there could be nothing new.

"These ancients knew that whatever was red was in essence heat, whatever was white was in essence water and whatever was black was in essence earth. Whatever seemed as un-known to them, they knew it as a compound of red, white and black essences.

"O' dear, now you learn from me as to how the three fundamental elements when bestowed consciousness by the presence of the Supreme Being further divide themselves in threes.

"The food when eaten divides itself in three parts: the coarse constituents become faeces, the medium ones turn into flesh and the finest of them makes the mind (or shapes the mind).

"The water when taken divides itself in three parts the coarse constituents becoming urine, the medium ones turn into blood and the finest of them form the life essence viz. the prāṇa.

"The energy-giving substances like fats (butter and oils) when consumed divide themselves in three parts: their coarse constituents become bones, the medium ones turn into marrow and the fines of them form the speech (vāk).

"So, my dear, the mind is made of food, the breath is made of water and speech is made of energy."

Spoke Śvetketu, "O' Venerable Sir, please instruct me further on this knowledge."

"So be it" Said Uddālaka Āruṇi.

"See O' dear, when milk in curd form is churned, its finest essence rises up to become the clarified butter (ghṛta). The same way, the finest essence of the eaten food rises up and becomes the mind. The finest essence of the taken water rises up and becomes the breath and the finest essence of the energy giving substances when consumed rises up and becomes speech.

"A person may survive without-eating food for a fortnight provided he continues taking sufficient water. This proves that life is sustained by water."

Ṛṣi Uddālaka then asked his son to keep a fast for a fortnight. On completion of fifteen days Śvetketu returned to his father and asked, "O' Venerable one, which chants should I recite?"

Said the father, "Recite to me the Ṛg, the Yajur and the Sāma Vedas of which you are well versed."

The youngman replied, "O' Respectable father, I can not recite all this because no chants come to my mind. It seems I have forgotten everything."

The sage explained, "Just as a small portion that remained kindled from an erstwhile great fire can not burn much, the sixteenth part[10] of your erstwhile energy will not be able to do much. Go and eat. Then alone will you understand the essence of my instruction."

As told, Śvetketu had had a good meal. Thereafter, he was able to answer the questions put to him by his father.

Spoke Āruṇi, "Just as a small portion that remained kindled from an erstwhile great fire when put to a heap of fire wood and helped to blaze was in a position to burn a great deal, even so could the sixteenth part of your energy when boosted through food could enable you to understand and recite the chants of the Vedas. All this was because O' dear son, mind is made of food, the breath is made of water and the speech is made of heat."

---

[10] That is to say, with your fasting for fifteen days you exhausted fifteen of the sixteen parts of your life-energy.

The son had understood the instruction so imparted by his father. But, Uddālaka Āruṇi had much more to teach yet. So, he continued with the discourse taking up the instruction regarding the state of sleep.

He spoke, "During the state of sound sleep, a person reaches the self. He is then known to have gone to his own (svapiti)."

"Like a bird fastened with a string flies here and flies there and finding no quarters settle down on to its string itself, so does the mind as fastened to the breath take its flight hither and thither but finding no quarters elsewhere eventually settles down on the breath itself. O' dear son, the breath is the controller of mind. (Prāṇabandhanam hi somey manaḥ[11].)

"O' son, now learn from me, the knowledge about hunger and thirst. When a person desires to eat he is called hungry. Or, when a person is hungry he desires to eat. The food so eaten is converted into liquid by water and led by it to various parts of the anatomy. This is why water is called the leader of food (āśnāya) as some one is called a leader of cows (gaunāya) or a leader of horses (aśvanāya) or a leader of people (puruṣanāya). And so know ye O' son, this body which is born of the eaten food is not without a root. Food is its root. From the food you know its (food's) root viz. water and from the water the root of the water viz. heat. From the heat you understand that the ultimate root is the Supreme Being (sat) alone. That alone is the root (moola) of all, is the quarter (āyatana) of all and is the foundation (pratiṣtĥa) of all.

---

11 In deed, this relationship between mind and breath is the basis of all yogic exercises.

"Similarly, when a person desires to drink water he is called thirsty. The consumed water is led to various parts of the body by heat. This is why heat is called the leader of water (udanāya) just as some one is called the leader of cows or a leader of horses or a leader of people. And so know ye O' Son, this body which is born like a sprout is not without a root. And what is its root? Heat is its root and since Supreme Being alone is the ultimate root all things are rooted and quartered in the Supreme Being alone.

"As made known earlier during the discourse, the three fundamental elements viz. heat, water and earth when bestowed with consciousness by the being (jivātmā) undergo the triple permutation-combination process so as to create a new form. But, when one is about to die, speech gets absorbed in mind, mind gets absorbed in breaths, breath gets absorbed in energy (tejaħ) and energy gets absorbed in the Great Lord (parama-devatā) that which is Infinite.

"The Infinite is the life (prāņa) of the whole universe. That alone is the self, That alone is the Self and thou That are, O'Śvetketu."

It seemed Śvetketu's mind was not yet at peace. Uddālaka, therefore, continued with his discourse.

"O' dear, like the juices of various fruit trees when collected and converted by the bees into a unified substance called honey do not there after know as to which particular tree they individually belonged even so these beings on merging into the Reality do not know that they have reached the ultimate. On the contrary, they cling on to their erstwhile identities. All such creatures like the tigers, lions, wolves, boars, worms, flies, gnats and mosquitoes are so born time and again because they do not shed their past. The infinitesimal soul (ātman) is the finest essence permeating the whole universe (or is the life-essence of the whole universe). That alone is the truth, that alone is the Self and, O' Śvetketu, thou That are."

Spoke the son, "O' Venerable Sir, Pray instruct me further on it."

'So, be it' said Uddālaka and proceeded to provide further examples of the unity of the self and the Self.

"O' dear, all these rivers that flow eastward or northward come from the ocean and eventually go to the ocean thereby becoming ocean themselves. Having attained ocean-ness (Samudratva) these rivers do not retain their separate identities. Verily, on the contrary all these living beings (the beings other than the humans) do not realize that they have come forth from Him alone. For this reason (or for this ignorance) they continue taking birth as tigers or lions or wolves or bears or worms or flies or gnats or mosquitees again and again. That Infinite is the source of the whole Universe. That alone is truth, That alone is the Self and O' Śvetketu, thou That are."

Pointing towards a tree the sage continued, "If some one were to strike with an axe at the root of this tree, it would bleed and not die. The same way, if some one were to strike at its middle portion or at its top it would bleed and not die. It is so, because so long as the life essence (jivātmā) permeates it, it will continue sucking food from the earth and stay alive. When the life essence leaves a branch of this tree, that branch turns dry, when it leaves the other branch, that particular branch too turns dry and so on. Eventually, when the life essence leaves the tree, as such, the whole tree dries up. The similar is the truth about the human body. Assuredly, when the soul leaves this body the latter alone dies and not the soul. The infinitesimal soul is the finest essence permeating the whole universe. That alone is truth, that alone is the Self and O' Śvetketu thou That are."

Then Uddālaka asked his son to fetch a fig fruit and break it. Śvetketu did as directed. Then the father asked, "What do you find inside?"

"The seeds." answered the youngman.

"Now break one of the seeds and let me know as to what lies inside the same," told the father. The son did as directed and reported that he saw nothing inside the seed.

Propounded the sage, "O' dear, the finest essence that you are unable to see in the seed is the cause of the great fig tree that you find standing thither. There is no doubt about that. So, this gross universe which you see has come forth from the Infinite which is most subtle, imperceptible and undescribable. That Infinite is the finest essence permeating the whole universe. That alone is truth that alone is the Self and O' Śvetketu, thou That are.'

Ṛṣi Uddālaka, then, asked his son to fetch a bowl of water, and put some salt in that and leave the vessel aside for the night. Next morning, getting the bowl brought to him the old man asked his son to take the salt out of the water. Śvetketu tried in vain to locate the salt which he himself had put in the water.

Spoke the father, "I shall tell you now as to how could one know that the salt was there in the water. Take a sip of the water from the top."

Śvetketu did as directed.

"How is it?" Asked the father.

"It is saltish," replied the son.

"Now take a sip of the water from the middle of the bowl," instructed Uddālaka.

Śvetketu did as directed.

"How is it?" Asked the father.

"It is saltish." Said the son.

"Now take a sip of the water from the bottom of the bowl." Uddālaka told his son.

Śvetketu did as directed.

"How is it?" The son replied, "O' Venerable Sir, the salt is there in the water all through."

Happy with his son's observation, Uddālaka exclaimed, "O' Son, as you knew not about the salt merely by looking at the water but came to know of its presence by tasting the water even so you cannot see the Infinite which is present everywhere and all the time. You can only realize Him[12]. That infinite is the finest essence permeating the whole Universe. That alone is truth, that alone is the Self and O' Śvetketu thou That are."

At this stage, Śvetketu requested that he be told about the true path leading one to the realization of the self.

Said Uddālaka, "O' dear, if a person is brought blind folded from the Gāndhāra country(presently in Afghanistan) and is dropped in a forest whether facing eastward, northward, downward or upward he would tell cryingly that he was brought blind-folded. Once the blind-folds are removed from his eyes and the direction of his destination is indicated to him, if he is knowledgeable and intelligent enough sooner or later he reaches his country, of course, on receiving further guidance from the people enroute. The same way, the infinitesimal soul is delayed in reaching the Infinite only so long as it remained shackled by the ignorance caused by this body. The Infinite is the finest essence permeating the whole Universe. That alone is truth, that alone is the Self and O' Śvetketu thou That are."

Concluding his discourse said Uddālaka, "O' dear, sitting around a dying person, the relatives ask him, "Do

---

12 For such a realization some efforts are necessary. These efforts include listening and reflecting about Him and observance of a code of daily routine.

you know me. Do you know me"? He knows this only so long as his speech does not pass into his mind, the mind into the breath,(prāṇa) the breath into the energy (tejaḥ) and the energy into the Brahma. But once it happens so, he no longer knows anything. The Brahma is the finest essence permeating the whole univers. That alone is truth, that alone is the Self and O', Śvetketu thou That are."

This is how Śvetketu came to acquire the subtle knowledge of the oneness of the self and the Self from his father.

Chhāndogyopaniṣad

PART TWO

Chapter 13

The Yājńvalkya Episode

The third and the fourth books of the Bṛhadāraṇykopaniṣad contain a highly illuminating series of discourses which taken together are known as the Yājńvalkya Kānda (the Yājńvalkya Episode) or the Muni Kānda. Yājńvalkya was a householder learned philosopher in the true Vedic tradition. He owned land, wealth and cattle. He was a man of great learning and had acquired expertise in the field of Vedic ritual and exegesis. - Yajnavalkya was the original teacher of White Yajurveda though he was a pupil of Vaishampāyana who was the original teacher of the Black Yajur-Veda.

As was customary during the period, he ran an educational institution which attracted students from all quarters. His prowess as a thinker and knower of Brahma was known far and wide providing him free access to the courts of contemporary kings where he participated in proceedings with great élan. Indeed, he dominates the teachings of the Bṛhadāraṇykopaniṣad and emerges as one of the main exponents of the Advaita philosophy. After discharging all his obligations as a householder and making adequate provisions for both of his wives he became a monk so as to practise his own teachings viz. 'for what need has he of offsprings whose self is the universe?'

Once, a great many scholars haling from the countries of Kurus and Pānchālas had assembled at the court of Janaka, the king of Videha. The occasion had gathered an added importance because the king had announced his intention of knowing as to who among the assembled Brāhmins was the most erudite scholar. As a prize for the winner, the king had ordered a thousand good cows, with as many as ten gold coins fastened onto the horns of each one of them, to be kept in a closeby enclosure. Addressing the august audience the king of Videha declared, "Venerable Brāhmins, let him who is the best Vedic scholar amongst you drive these cows home."

The reward indeed was big enough! But no less big was the challenge. The Vedic lore being immeasurably vast, who would dare arrogate to himself the position of the knower of it all? With Yājńvalkya, however, matters were different. Not only was he well-versed with the contents of the Vedas, he was also a competent debater. Finding everyone present in the assembly perplexed by the royal announcement, he got up and directed one of his pupils to drive the cows' home.

Obviously, this stirred up the hornets' nest and scholar after scholar rose to challenge Yājńvalkya. Thus, a great debate commenced immortalizing the sage Yājńvalkya and his benefactor, the Videha King.

Asvala, the chief priest of the king was the first interlocutor, who put questions on the subject of Vedic rituals. The essence of the answers provided by Yājńvalkya, in response, was that the result of rituals and sacrifices performed for obtaining material gains was rebirth of the doer so that the corresponding rewards could be enjoyed. But, if the ritual sacrifices were performed alongwith the prescribed meditations the reward was liberation from the cycle of births and deaths.

The next scholar who rose to ask questions was Ārtabhāga. The teaching of this part of the discourse is that once a person frees himself from identification with the perishable sense-organs as also from their objects through the knowledge of the self, he on casting off this body merges with the Brahma.

Bhujyu was the next scholar who intervened. He was told that all attainments in the phenomenal world including attainment of the world of Prajāpati (Prajāpati-loka) were inherently impermanent because all such rewards were the outcome of actions (Karmas) which by their nature were temporary. The ultimate liberation from the phenomenal world was possible only through the knowledge of Brahma. The scholar held his peace.

Uṣasta's question, who was the next speaker, pertained to the definition of the in-dwelling individual self viz. the infinitesimal self. Yājńvalkya explained that the entity which directs and controls various prāṇas in the body is the individual self. This self, because of its identification with the senses and attachment to their objects gets subjected to decay or death, as it were. This prompted another scholar, Kahola by name, to raise a question about the Infinite Self. We are told by Yājńvalkya that since the Infinite or the Supreme Self is beyond all identifications and attachments, it is beyond all wants, pains, decay or death. So, the Supreme Self can be known only by renouncing all desires and attachments.

Gārgi, a woman philosopher, then challenged Yājńvalkya to demonstrate the Ultimate Reality through the logic of causality. In an erudite manner, the sage drove home the point that the logic of causality was relevant only with reference to the phenomenal world. Since, the

Ultimate Reality is beyond the reach of reason it can not be so demonstrated. The Supreme Reality, he added, could be known only on the authority of the revelations as contained in the scriptures. Gārgi held her peace, though only for the time being.

Uddālaka was the next questioner. He tested Yājńvalkya's depth of knowledge with regard to the subtler issues concerning relationship among various phenomena of creation and between the phenomenal world and the Ultimate Reality. His inquiry was three fold viz. what is the support and essence of all elements? What is that thread by which all phenomenal entities are held together? And who was the Inner controller of all beings? Yājńvalkya told the great assembly that the Hiraṇyagarbha is the support of all elements and so is the essence of the entire universe. The Hiraṇyagarbha also is the thread (Sutra) which holds all the phenomenal entities together. The Inner Controller (Antaryāmin) of all beings however, is the Self." The interlocutor then held his peace.

Gārgi, the woman philosopher aforementioned, wanted to know as to what pervaded the thread (Sutra) that pervaded all beings. Yājńvalkya informed her that the Imperishable Brahma, as described by the scriptures through negation of all attributes, pervaded the thread that pervades all beings. After listening to Yājńvalkya who was expositing such subtle issues so effortlessly Gārgi declared that to defeat him in the debate was not possible.

That however did not deter sage Śakala from asking questions with regard to various divinities. He was told that God is one though meditated upon differently by different people. All such worshippers acquire different levels in mental and spiritual attainments which correspond to their level of meditation. He further stated that all divinities are part of the Hiraṇyagarbha alone and that the names and forms ascribed to these divinities are descriptive of their assigned functions.

The end of the debate was not happy for sage Śakala as he lost his head for not providing an answer to counter-question asked by Yājńvalkya.

Thus, Muni Yājńvalkya proved his mettle by providing appropriate answers to all his challengers. In the end, all the assembled scholars accepted his supremacy as knower of the Vedic lore. The sage then drove away the prized cows triumphantly to his hermitage. Of this episode, only three of Yājńvalkya's dialogues viz. two with Gārgi and one with Uddālaka are included in the present work.

Book four of the Bṛhadāraṇykopaniṣad contains primarily Yājńvalkya's discourses to king Janaka on questions relating to the Ultimate Unity, the infinitesimal self and the Infinite Self. The grand finale of the Munikānd is reached when in his dialogue with his younger spouse Maitreyi the sage sums up the philosophy of Advaita Vedānta (Non-Duality) before renouncing the world to become a sanyāsin.

Chapter 14

The Self as the Warp And Woof of the Whole Universe

The first dialogue with Gārgi

Prolegomena

Once in the court ofJanaka Vaideha the sage Yājńvalkya's claim of being the greatest Vedic scholar was challenged by several reputed philosophers of the time. One of such challengers was Gārgi, the illustrious daughter of Vāchaknu. She was known for her vast knowledge, deeper understanding, and competent erudition. For these reasons she had made for herself a proud place amongst contemporary scholars. The earlier questions of the learned Brāhmins had primarily focused on details of the Vedic rituals. Some of them had spoken with regards to the definitions of the self and the Self. But she took up issues of far more subtle nature.

The Dialogue

Gārgi: "Yājńvalkya, since all this world is woven warp and woof (otam-protam)[1] on water(āpaħ)[2], on what is the water so woven?"

Yājńvalkya, "On air (Vāyu) O' Gārgi."

Gārgi, "On what is then the air woven warp and woof?"

Yājńvalkya, "On the space (antariksa-lok) O' Gārgi."

Gārgi, "On what is then the space woven warp and woof?"

Yājńvalkya, "On the world of Gandharvas[3] (Gandharva loka) O'Gārgi."

Gārgi, "On what is then the world of Gandharvas woven warp and woof?"

Yājńvalkya, "On the world of the Sun (āditya loka), O'Gārgi."

Gārgi, "On what is then the world of the sun woven warp and woof?"

Yājńvalkya. "On the world of the moon (Chandra loka), O'Gārgi."

Gārgi, "On what is then the world of the moon woven warp and woof?"

Yājńvalkya "Onthe world of stars (Naksatraloka), O' Gārgi."

Gārgi, "On what is then the world of the stars woven warp and woof?"

Yājńvalkya, "On the world of the gods (Devaloka), O' Gārgi."

---

1 That is to say, pervaded by.

2 "Otherwise the earth would be scattered like a handful of fried barley flour." Śankarāchārya.

3 The Gandharvas are the celestial beings between humans and the gods.

Gārgi, "On what is the world of the gods woven, warp and woof?"

Yājńvalkya, "On the world of Indra (Indra Loka), O' Gārgi."

Gārgi, "On what is the world of Indra woven, warp and woof?"

Yājńvalkya, "On the world of Prajāpati (Prajāpati Loka), O' Gārgi."

Gārgi, "On what is the world of Prajāpati woven, warp and woof?".

Yājńvalkya, "On the world of Brahma (Brahma Loka), O' Gārgi."

Gārgi, "On what is the world of Brahma woven, warp and woof?"

Yājńvalkya, "O' Gārgi, Do not ask too much lest your head should fall off. You are questioning too much about the deity of whom too much should not be asked. Do not ask too much, O' Gārgi."

One may infer from the response of Yājńvalkya that either the sage had become impatient with his questioner or that he was left with no answer.

Actually, neither was the case. The answers provided by the sage to Gārgi upto the position with regard to the worlds of Prajāpati could be ascertained either on the authority of logic or on the evidence of scriptures. And, both logic and acceptance of evidence are within the scope of mind. But, Brahma is beyond mind and can not be reasoned out. Therefore, Yājńvalkya cautioned Gārgi against pursuing her inquiry any further unless she wished to die.

[See, "We do not know—neither the sophists, nor the orators, nor the artists, nor I—what the true, the good, and the beautiful are. But there is this difference between us: Although these people know nothing, they all believe they know something; whereas, I, if I know nothing, at least have no doubt about it. I am strongly convinced that I am ignorant of what I do not know." Socrates]

There upon, Gārgi Vāchaknavi held her peace. She had known that 'On the world of Brahma all the worlds are woven warp and woof.'

* * *

The questions raised by Gārgi belonged to the realm of cause and effect with the well-established pre-suppositions that the effect is pervaded by the cause, that the limited is pervaded by the unlimited and that the gross is pervaded by the subtle. The teaching of the parable is that while the cause is pervaded by the subtle and the unlimited the effect is pervaded by the gross and the limited. Even the cause and effect are so interwoven that a particular cause at a certain link in the chain is the effect of the one proceeding in regression. And, thus the regressus ad infinitum takes one to the realization of Ultimate Reality.

Chapter 15

Breath As The Thread And Self as The Inner Controller

Dialogue with Uddālaka Āruṇi

Prolegomena

During the discourse at the court of King Janaka Vaideha referred to in the earlier parable, once Vāchaknavi Gārgi withdrew from the debate, though for the time being, Uddālaka, the son of Aruṇa joined issues with Yājṅvalkya. He raised questions with regard to the force that holds all elements of the creation together and about the power that regulates their functioning.

The centripetal cosmic energy which holds this limitless universe together and the power which regulates the functioning of all elements from within have been the objects of contemplation for thinkers of all ages and of all places. Verily, Yājṅvalkya could hardly lay claim to all knowledge if he did not know of these matters.

At this juncture, a recall to one of the fundamental assumptions of the Vedānta philosophy would be relevant.

It is believed that each of the element or phenomenon of the universe is animated by a particular divinity which also is identified with a corresponding organ of the human body. Accordingly, the phenomena like the earth, sun, moon, water, air and ether and the organs of the human body like eyes, ears and nose, all being gross in nature, have a particular divinity identified with each. These divinities are known by the name of the phenomenon or the organ concerned. As for example, the blazing orb in the sky known as the sun is a gross phenomenon which is inhabited by the divinity with the same name viz. the sun (āditya). Thus, the universe is visualized as an aggregate of innumerable divinities carrying out their assigned tasks. The questions which arise from such a hypothesis are, firstly, what force holds all these entities together and secondly, what power compels them to function in accordance with a precise and rigorous law?

The Parable

Uddālaka Āruṇi Said, "Yājńvalkya, when we were living in the house of Patanchala Kāpya in Madradesa for the purpose of studying the scriptures, it came to pass that the lady of the house was possessed by a Gandharva named Kabandha, the son of Atharvaṇa. That Gandharva once asked Patanchala and all of us who were his disciples, 'O, you the descendants of Kapi, do you know that thread (sutra) by which this world, the other worlds and all beings are held together? Patanchala replied in the negative. Again, the Gandharva asked, 'O, you the descendants of Kapi, do you know that Inner Controller (Antaryāmin) who from within controls this world, the other worlds and all the beings? Patanchala Kāpya said, 'O' Venerable Sir, I do not know." The Gandharva then said, "He who knows that thread and that Inner Controller indeed is knower of the Brahma (Brahma-vetā), is the knower of the Vedas (Veda-vetā) is the knower of beings (bhuta-vetā) and is the knower of everything (serva-vetā).."

Then he (the Gandharva), instructed all those who were present with regard to that Thread and that Inner Controller. I know all that. O' Yājńvalkya, if you do not know that and yet drive away the cows which are promised for the knower of the Brahma, your head shall fall."

Yājńvalkya replied, "O' Gautama[1], I know that Thread and that Inner Controller."

Retorted Uddālaka, "Anyone can say "I know', 'I know.' If you indeed know, then you tell."

Yājńvalkya, "Air (Vāyu), O' Gautama is that Thread[2]. By air O' Gautama, as by a thread, are held together this world, the other worlds and all beings. Therefore, O' Gautama, it is said of a dead person that his limbs have become unstrung (Visirṇa) for, by Vāyu O' Gautama, as by a thread are they strung together (Sangrahit). Uddālaka said, "O Yājńvalkya, quite so. Now you tell about the Inner Controller,"

Yājńvalkya, "He who inhabits the earth and is within the earth, whom the earth does not know, whose body earth is and who controls the earth from within He is your[3] Self, the Inner Controller, the Immortal."

---

[1] This is Uddālaka's family epithet (gotra).

[2] In the context, Vāyu signifies the prāna viz. the Cosmic Life Breath. As per the Vedic belief the Hiraṇyagarbha (the Brahma personified) is the life breath of the entire universe.

[3] A reference to Self or Self or Soul when made in either of the person; second or third (your or his) means the Self or soul of all others as well.

"He who inhabits water and is within water, who water does not know, whose body water is and who controls the water from within He is your Soul, the Inner Controller, the Immortal."

"He who inhabits fire and is within fire, who fire does not know, whose body fire is and who controls the fire from within He is your Soul, the Inner Controller, the Immortal."

"He who inhabits space and is within space, who space does not know, whose body space is and who controls the space from within He is your Soul, the Inner Controller, the Immortal."

"He who inhabits air and is within air, who air does not know, whose body air is and who controls the air from within He is your Soul, the Inner Controller, the Immortal."

"He who inhabits heaven and is within heaven, who heaven does not know, whose body heaven is and who controls the heaven from within He is your Soul, the Inner Controller, the Immortal."

"He who inhabits sun and is within sun, who sun does not know, whose body sun is and who controls the sun from within He is your Soul, the Inner Controller, the Immortal."

"He who inhabits quarters and is within quarters, who quarters do not know, whose body quarters are and who controls the quarters from within He is your Soul, the Inner Controller, the Immortal."

"He who inhabits moon and the stars and is within moon and the stars, whom the moon and the stars do not know whose body moon and the stars are and who controls the moon and the stars from within He is your Soul, the Inner Controller, the Immortal."

"He who inhabits sky and is within sky, who sky does not know, whose body sky is and who controls the sky from within He is your Soul, the Inner Controller, the Immortal."

"He who inhabits darkness and is within darkness, who darkness does not know, whose body darkness is and who controls the darkness from within He is your Soul, the Inner Controller, the Immortal."

"He who inhabits light and is within light, whom light does not know, whose body light is and who controls the light from within He is your Soul, the Inner Controller, the Immortal."

"This much philosophy is with reference to gods (adhidaivata darśan) and now the philosophy with reference to material existence (adhibhoota-darśan)." [Adhibhoot refers to all beings ranging from Brahmā or Hiraṇyagarbha to the clump of grass (Brahmādistamba paryantesu).

"He who inhabits all beings and is within all beings, whom all beings do not know, whose body all beings are and who controls all beings from within He is your Soul, the Inner Controller, the Immortal.

"This much philosophy is with reference to the material existence and now the philosophy with reference to the Self (adhiātman).

"He, who dwells in the breath (prāṇa), yet is within the breath, who the breath does not know, whose body the breath is and who controls the breath from within He is your Soul, the Inner Controller, the Immortal."

"He, who dwells in the speech (vāk), yet is within the speech, who the speech does not know, whose body the speech is and who controls the speech from within He is your Soul, the Inner Controller, the Immortal."

"He, who dwells in the eye (chakṣu), yet is within the eye, who the eye does not know, whose body the eye is and who controls the eye from within He is your Soul, the Inner Controller, the Immortal."

"He, who dwells in the ear (śrotra), yet is within the ear, who the ear does not know, whose body the ear is and who controls the ear from within He is your Soul, the Inner Controller, the Immortal."

"He, who dwells in the mind (manas), yet is within the mind, who the mind does not know, whose body the mind is and who controls the mind from within He is your Soul, the Inner Controller, the Immortal."

"He, who dwells in the skin (tvaka), yet is within the skin, who the skin does not know, whose body the skin is and who controls the skin from within He is your Soul, the Inner Controller, the Immortal."

"He, who dwells in the intellect (Vijńānam)[4], yet is within the intellect, who the intellect does not know, whose body the intellect is and who controls the intellect from within He is your Soul, the Inner Controller, the Immortal."

"He, who dwells in the semen (retaħ), yet is within the semen, who the semen does not know, whose body the semen is and who controls the semen from within He is your Soul, the Inner Controller, the Immortal."

---

[4] The term intellect in the Vedic context does not refer to brain, but to true knowledge. Similarly, the term Vijnana in the vedic context refers to superior/special/specific knowledge and not to 'science' as is understood today. Otherwise as well there exists a close relationship between spirituality and science."

Science is not only compatible with spirituality; it is a profound source of spirituality. When we recognize our place in immensity of light years and in the passage of ages, when we grasp the intricacy, beauty and subtlety of life, then that soaring feeling, that sense of elation and humility combined, is surely spiritual. So are our emotions in the presence of great or music or literature, or acts of exemplary selfless courage." J Carl Sagan. American author.

"He is the unseen, but is the seer; He is the unheard, but is the hearer; He is the unthought but is the thinker; He is the unknown, but is the knower. There is no seer other than Him; there is no hearer other than Him; there is no thinker other than Him; there is no knower other than Him. He is your soul, the Inner Controller, the Immortal. All else is perishable.

Thereupon, Uddālaka, the son of Aruṇa, asked no more questions.

* * *

The logic of the dialogue is sustained by the belief that the Ultimate Reality (the Brahma) has no body or organ of Its own and that all organs in the case of a human body and all elements and phenomena in the case of the cosmic body are inhabited by the divinities identified with them and that all these divinities perform their allotted functions as per the Divine Law (The Dharma).

The teaching of the Upaniṣad here is two-fold; firstly, the Cosmic Life Breath (Prāṇa or the Hiraṇyagarbha) is the Thread (Sutra) that holds all beings together and secondly, the immortal soul (the Ātman) which dwells within each being is its Inner Controller. Both of these entities viz. the life breath and the transmigrating soul are aspects of Conditioned Brahma (Hiraṇyagarbha or Saguṇa Brahma). Hiraṇyagarbha (the Manifest Brahma) has both individual and aggregate aspects. In the individual mode it supports each individual being and in the aggregate mode it pervades the whole creation, thus keeping all beings strung together like a thread that so keeps all the pearls in a necklace. The transmigrating soul too belongs to the Manifest Brahma (called the universe), the attendant body being its limiting adjunct (upādhi) as projected by illusion or ignorance (the māyā). These limiting aspects are seen in the perspective of time and space, creating the illusion of separatedness from the rest. Our feelings and thoughts, as it were, create the delusion of consciousness me and mine. The task or goal or purpose, say what you may, of human life is to rise above these petty feelings so as to expand our horizon and seek oneness with the Ultimate Reality, the Braham.

By making a reference to 'ignorance' (the māyā), in the dialogue the Upanişad has described the Manifest Brahma or the Conditioned Brahma as the sustaining and regulatory force of the universe.

Chapter 16

The Attribute less Supreme Being is The Ultimate Inner Controller of the Universe

The Second Dialogue with Gārgi

Prolegomena

It may be recalled that during her earlier encounter, Gārgi was cautioned by the sage Yājńvalkya against raising too many questions about the One of whom too much must not be asked. Perhaps, at that stage she had withdrawn from the debate to avoid unpleasant consequences attendant to such an inquiry. To ward off such eventuality she took extra care and obtained permission of learned Brāhmins for proceeding further with her questioning of Yājńvalkya.

As noted earlier in the dialogue with the sage Uddālaka the Upaniṣad had imparted instruction with regard to the Conditioned Brahma. In the present dialogue the instruction proceeds further so as to describe the Unconditioned

Supreme Being. The dialogue also creates some dramatic effects.

The Dialogue

Gārgi said, "Venerable Brāhmins, now I shall ask him two questions. If he gives me answers to these, then no one amongst you will be able to defeat him in the debate on Brahma."

The Brāhmins: "Ask, O' Gārgi."

Gārgi: "O' Yājńvalkya, as a scion of a brave family of Kāśi or Videha might confront his foe with two highly pain-inflicting arrows and a well-strung bow, so do I stand before you with two questions. Pray answer them."

Yājńvalkya: "Ask O' Gārgi".

Gārgi: "O' Yājńvalkya, what pervades that which is above the heaven and below the earth that which is between the heaven and the earth, that which is heaven and earth[1] and which they[2] say was, is and will be?"

Yājńvalkya, "O' Gārgi, that which is above the heaven and below the earth, that which is between the heaven and the earth and that which is heaven and earth and which they say was, is and will be is pervaded by the space[3](ākāśa).

---

[1] All this describes the Manifest. The heaven and earth respectively represent the upper and lower halves of the Cosmic Shell, the Hiraṇyagarbha.

[2] They say' stands for the scriptures.

[3] Śankarāchārya explains it as the Un-manifest ākāśa comprising the Thread viz. the Hiraṇyagarbha that exists in the Unmanifest (ākāśa) at all times; during the stages of creation, preservation and dissolution.

Gārgi: "I bow to you, O' Yājńvalkya for providing answer to my first question. Pray, be prepared to answer my second question."

Yājńvalkya; "Ask O' Gārgi."

Gārgi: "O' Yājńvalkya, what pervades that which is above the heaven and below the earth that which is heaven and earth and which they say was, is and will be?"

Yājńvalkya: "O' Gārgi, that which is above the heaven and below the earth, that which is between the heaven and the earth and that which is heaven and earth and which they say was, is and will be pervaded by space."

Gārgi: "But what pervades the space."

[Gārgi had used her final arrow with dexterity so as to put her opponent in a dilemma. The Unmanifested Ākāśa is pervaded by none other than the Brahma Itself which is unexplainable. In the given situation if Yājńvalkya did not explain the 'One that pervades the Thread' then it would be held that he did not know the answer (logic of non comprehension); on the other hand should he dare make an effort to explain the unexplainable he would be held guilty of attempting to do some thing impossible (the logic of contradiction). But, Yājńvalkya was a past-master in the game. Besides being one of the finest metaphysical thinkers of all times, he was an erudite debater. He, therefore, answered the question by quoting the knowers of Brahma as his authority and by describing the Brahma in the negative terms viz. neither this nor that. Thus, he incurred no infringement of logic].

Yājńvalkya: 'O, Gārgi, the knowers of the Brahma call that 'the Imperishable[4] (Akşara-Brahma); It is neither gross

---

[4] The expression Akşara-Brahma means that which does not change or decay.

nor subtle, neither small nor big, neither red nor moist, neither shadow nor darkness, neither air nor sky. It is unattached, odourless, and tasteless, without eyes, without ears, without speech, without air, without energy, without breath, without mouth, without measure, without inside and without outside. It consumes naught, no one ever consumes It."

He then hastened to add[5] "O' Gārgi, under the mighty dispensation of this Imperishable One, sun and moon stay in their pre-determined positions. Under the mighty dispensation of this Imperishable One heaven and earth are held in their pre-determined positions. O' Gārgi, under the mighty dispensation of this Imperishable One moments, muhurtas[6], days and nights, fortnights, months, seasons and years are held in their pre-determined positions. Under the mighty dispensation of this Imperishable One the rivers that issue forth from snow clad mountain peaks maintain their directions eastward or westward as ordained. O' Gārgi, in the mighty dispensation of this Imperishable One men praise those who give, the gods depend upon the oblations offered through sacrifices and the fathers upon their exclusive offerings (darvi-homa).

"Without knowing this Imperishable One, O' Gārgi, whosoever in this world offers oblations, performs sacrifices and meditates for thousands of years finds all such acts perishable. Whosoever leaves this world without knowing this Imperishable One remains miserable[7] and, O' Gārgi whosoever leaves this world having known this Imperishable One is knower of Brahma".

---

5 This was necessary to avoid creating the misconception that in that case Brahma might be a void or non-existent.

6 Denotes time.

7 Because of the cycle of deaths and births.

"Verily, O' Gārgi, this Imperishable One is not seen but is the seer, is not heard but is the hearer is not the object of thought but is the thinker. It is never known but is the knower of all. There is no seer other than this, there is no hearer other than this; there is no thinker other than this and there is no knower other than this. Verily, O' Gārgi, this space is pervaded by this Imperishable One."

Gārgi's Judgment

Declared Gārgi, "Venerable Brāhmins, you may consider yourself lucky should you escape from him (Yājńvalkya) only by paying obeisance. Not one of you will ever defeat him in a disputation on Brahma."

There upon, she held her peace.

* * *

Teaching

Infact Yājńvalkya's dialogues with Uddālaka and Gārgi are complementary to each other. In both the discourses the Inner Controller has been described. While with Uddālaka it is the transmigrating ātman, with Gārgi it is the Imperishable One. The ātman of Uddālaka hales from the Manifest or the Conditioned Brahma (the Saguṇa Brahma). The Imperishable One, on the other hand, is an aspect of the Unconditioned Reality (the Nirguṇa Brahma). The difference between the two is not intrinsic but is an outcome of the association of the saguṇa with the limiting adjuncts (upādhis). The ultimate teaching of the Upaniṣads stays as "One, without a second."

Chapter 17

The Self as the Abode And Support of All

Dialogue with King Janaka

Prolegomena

The venu of this discourse is the court of the Vedeha king. During the earlier encounter in the assembly of the Vedic scholars Yājńvalkya had described Brahma from the standpoints of Saguṇa and Nirguṇa. That discourse had culminated into the instruction that the Ultimate Reality was One, without a second, as could be described in negative terms viz. 'not-this,' not-this'. It was also stated that the Nirguṇa Brahma possessed no organ or body of Its own. Instead, all cosmic phenomena and the knowledge organs of the human body were animated by specific divinities which function under His mighty dispensation working in his behalf and for serving His purpose. This statement, however, needed a detailed contemplation.

The dialogue that follows imparts instruction with regard to Brahma with reference to the various divinities.

Since there were no other questioners present on the occasion, Yājńvalkya was free from the stress for proving his scholarship, as was the case earlier. Consequently, the discourse proceeds in the form of a dialogue between a seeker viz. the king Janaka and a knower of truth viz. the sage Yājńvalkya. This dialogue also signifies the transformation of Vaideha Janaka from a philosopher amongst kings to a king amongst philosophers.

The Dialogue

Once when Janaka Vaideha was getting ready for giving audience, the renowned sage Yājńvalkya entered his chambers. After the usual exchange of courtesies the king asked, "O' Yājńvalkya, with what purpose do you come? Is it for the cattle or for a discourse on some subtle issues?"[1]

[It indeed was an awkward question. Perhaps, the king had Yājńvalkya's earlier visit to his court in mind when the latter had walked away with as many as one thousand cows as a trophy. The sage however kept his cool. It seems he was aware of the royal ego that made Janaka place the cattle at par with the discussion on the subtle issues of philosophy. The right course for Yājńvalkya to adopt therefore was to relieve the king of such misconceptions in an appropriate manner. That was what he actually proceeded to do. All the same, the question also shows that the king was aware of the capabilities of his learned visitor who was equally deft in tackling scholarly challenges as also in indulging in serious discourses without a desire for rewards.]

Yājńvalkya: "For both, Your Majesty." Then he added, "Let me hear what other teachers have told you."

---

1 Perhaps, it was a comment made in a lighter vein. But, the sage converted it into an opportunity to deliver a message.

Janaka: "Jitvā, the son of Śilina, told me that speech (vāk) is Brahma."[2]

Yājńvalkya, "As any one who had been instructed well by mother, father and teacher[3] should say what the son of Śilina said. The divinity of speech is Brahma. Obviously, what can one who does not have the facility of speech attain? But did he tell you what were the abode (āyatana) and support (pratiṣṭhā) of the divinity of speech?

Janaka, "No, he did not tell me that."

Yājńvalkya "O' King, this Brahma is only one footed."

[Meaning thereby, the answer was not complete. It is only a quarter of the whole answer.]

Janaka: "Pray, you tell me about that."

Yājńvalkya: "The organ of speech is its abode and the sky (ākāśa) is its support. It should be meditated upon as Intelligence (Prajnā).

Janaka: "What is Intelligence O' Yājńvalkya?"

Yājńvalkya: "The speech, Your Majesty, is Intelligence. Through speech alone are known the Ṛgveda, the Yajurveda, the Sāmaveda, the Atharvangirāsa, history, Purāṇas, arts, Upaniṣads, verses, aphorisms, explanations, commentaries, the attainments of sacrifices (iṣta), the attainments of oblations (huta), the merits earned by giving food to a hungry person (asita) and drink to a thirsty person (payita) this world, the world yonder and all beings.

"O' king, speech alone is the Supreme Brahma. He who knowing this meditates on it so, the divinity of speech never deserts him, all beings offer him gifts, and becoming godlike on earth he attains the gods after death."

Janaka: "I give a thousand cows which will produce bulls as large as elephants."

---

2 Speech is identified with the fire-god (Agni-devatā)

3 These are the three teachers of a person.

Yājńvalkya: "My father was of the view that a teacher should not accept gifts from a disciple without instructing him to his (disciple's) satisfaction. Let me hear what anyone from amongst your teachers may have told you."

Janaka: "Udaņka, the son of Śulba, has told me that the Vital Breath (Prāņa) alone is Brahma."

Yājńvalkya: "As anyone who has been instructed well by mother, father and teacher should say what the son of Śulbha said. The Vital Breath (the Mukhya Prāņa) is Brahma because what can one who does not breathe attain? But did he tell you what were the abode and support of the Vital Breath?"

Janaka: "No he did not tell me that."

Yājńvalkya: "O' king, this Brahma is only one-footed,"

Janaka: "Pray, you tell me about that."

Yājńvalkya: "The Vital Breath is its abode and sky, (ākāśa) is its support. It should be meditated upon as Dear (Priya)".

Janaka: "What is that dearness (priyatā) O' Yājńvalkya?"

Yājńvalkya, "O' Emperor, the vital breath[4] is dearness. For the sake of vital breath only are sacrifices performed for him for whom they should not be performed; gifts are accepted from whom they should not be accepted. For the sake of vital breath, O king, one even dares to go to a place where one runs the risk of life. All this is done for the sake of vital breath, O' king.

"The vital breath is the Supreme Brahma. He who knowing this meditates on it so, the vital breath never deserts him, all beings offer him gifts, and becoming godlike on earth he attains gods after death."

Janaka: "I give you a thousand cows which will produce bulls as large as elephants."

---

[4] The vital breath is identified with the air-god (Vāyu devatā).

Yājńvalkya: "My father was of the view that a teacher should not accept gifts from a disciple without instructing him to his (disciple's) satisfaction. Let me hear what anyone from amongst your teachers may have told you."

Janaka: "Barku, the son of Vṛṣṇa, has told me that the light (chakṣu) alone is Brahma."[5]

Yājńvalkya: "As anyone who has been instructed well by mother, father and teacher should say what the son of Vṛṣṇa said. The sight is Brahma because what can one who does not see attain? But did he tell you what were the abode and support of the sight?

Janaka: "No, he did not tell me that."

Yājńvalkya: "O' king, this Brahma is only one-footed."

Janaka: "Pray, you tell me about that."

Yājńvalkya: "The eye is its abode and the sky is its support. It should be meditated upon as True.

Janaka: "What is this truthfulness O' Yājńvalkya?"

Yājńvalkya: "O' king, the eye alone is true. When one is asked, 'Have you seen?' and the answer is 'yes' then it is taken as true. The sight is the Supreme Brahma. He who knowing this, meditates on it so, the sight never deserts him, all beings offer him gifts, and becoming godlike on earth he attains gods after death.'

Janaka: "I give you a thousand cows which will produce bulls as large as elephants."

Yājńvalkya: "My father was of the opinion that a teacher should not accept gifts from a disciple without instructing him to his satisfaction.

Let me hear what anyone from amongst your teachers may have told you."

---

5 The sight is identified with the sun-god.

Janaka: "Gardabhivipeeta of the Bhardwāja family has told me that 'hearing' (śrotra) alone is Brahma."[6]

Yājńvalkya: "As anynone who has been instructed well by mother, father and teacher should say what the scion of the Bharadwāj family said. The hearing is Brahma because what can one who does not hear attain? But did he tell you what were the abode and support of hearing?'

Janaka: "No, he did not tell me that."

Yājńvalkya: "O' king, this Brahma is one footed."

Janaka: "Pray, you tell me about that."

Yājńvalkya: "The ear is its abode and the sky is its support. It should be meditated upon as Infinite."

Yājńvalkya: "O' Emperor, the quarters (directions) are alone infinite. Whatever quarters one goes to, one never reaches its end because quarters are infinite and quarters are hearing. Hearing is the Supreme Brahma. He who knowing this, meditates upon it so, the hearing never deserts him, all beings offer him gifts, and becoming god-like on earth, he attains gods after death."

Janaka: "I give a thousand of cows which will produce bulls as large as elephants."

Yājńvalkya: "My father was of the view that a teacher should not accept gifts from a disciple without instructing him to his satisfaction.

Let me hear what anyone from amongst your teachers may have told you?"

Janaka: "Satyakāma, the son of Jabālā, has told me that mind (manas) alone is Brahma.[7]

Yājńvalkya: "As anyone who has been instructed well by mother, father and teacher should say what the son of Jabālā said. The mind alone is Brahma because what can

---

6 The hearing is identified with the god of directions.

7 The mind is identified with the moon-god.

one who does not have mind attain? But did he tell you what were the abodes and support of mind?

Janaka: "No, he did not tell me that."

Yājńvalkya: "O' king, this Brahma is one-footed."

Janaka: "Pray, you tell me about that."

Yājńvalkya: "Mind is its abode and the sky is its support. It should be meditated upon as Bliss."

Janaka: "What is this blissfulness O' Yājńvalkya?"

Yājńvalkya: "O' Emperor, mind alone is blissfulness. O' king, because of the mind alone one desires to betake a woman, then a son (progeny) resembling him is born, that is bliss! O' Emperor, mind alone is the Supreme Brahma. He who knowing this meditates upon it so, the mind never deserts him, all beings offer him gifts, becoming god-like on earth, he attains gods after death,"

Janaka: "I give a thousand cows which will produce bulls as large as elephants."

Yājńvalkya: "My father was of the view that a teacher should not accept gifts from a disciple without instructing him to his satisfaction.

Let me hear what anyone from amongst your teachers may have told you?"

Janaka: "Vidagdha Śākalya has told me that heart (hṛdaya) alone is Brahma.[8]

Yājńvalkya: "As anyone who has been instructed well by mother, father and teacher should say what the son of Śakala said, "The heart alone is Brahma because what can one who does not have heart attain? But did he tell you what were the abodes and support of heart?"

Janaka: "No, he did not tell me that."

Yājńvalkya: "O' king, this Brahma is one-footed."

Janaka: "Pray, you tell me about that."

---

[8] The heart is identified with the Creater (Prajāpati).

Yājńvalkya: "Heart is its abode and the sky is its support. It should be meditated upon as Stability."

Janaka: "What is this stability O' Yājńvalkya?"

Yājńvalkya: "Heart alone is stability, O' Emperor. Heart is the abode of all beings and heart alone is the support of all beings. O' Emperor, heart alone is the Supreme Brahma. He who knowing this, meditates upon it so, the heart never deserts him, all beings offer him gifts, becoming god-like on earth, and he attains gods after death."

At this, Janaka left his regal seat, approached Yājńvalkya with all humility and after paying obeisance said, "Pray instruct me into the lore of the Self, the lore of the Brahma."

Yājńvalkya: "Your Majesty, as one who is about to leave for a long journey would obtain a chariot (in case he plans to move on land) or a boat (in case he is to move over water bodies) so you have fully provisioned your mind with the knowledge and worships of so many aspects of Brahma. Besides, you have acquired a niche of honour and wealth for yourself and have studied the Vedas and heard the Upanişads from teachers. But, do you know where will you go when released from this body?"

[The kind of chariot or the boat alone will not take you far. The king was well versed in the religious lore but he did not have the knowledge of Self and therefore, could not overcome the fear of death.]

Janaka: "Venerable Sir, I do not know where I shall go after leaving this body."[9]

Yājńvalkya: "Forsooth, if you do not know, then I will tell you where you will go."

Janaka: "Tell me, Venerable Sir."

Yājńvalkya: "Listen to me, then."

---

[9] That is to say that the king conceded that he had the fear of the unknown.

[The discourse so far was devoted to the partial descriptions of Brahma and the respective meditations (upāsanās). In what now follows, Brahma will be described with reference to the waking, dreaming and the deep sleep stages. Janaka, as is the wont of powerful and wealthy people, was arrogant when he awkwardly questioned the purpose of Yājńvalkya's visit. Finding that the sage was more than a match to all his previous preceptors, his ego dissipated. On the other hand, Yājńvalkya found, too, the time ripe enough for providing to the king a wholesome knowledge of the Self. Consequently, the discourse henceforth turned into a one-sided affair.]

Yājńvalkya: "The puruṣa in the right eye is known as Indha or Satya. This is his direct name as he is resplendent beauty. The devas call him Indra. They derive pleasure in being indirect; nay they dislike being direct. By knowing him (the Indra) you will know the self as Vaiśvānara, the waking stage. The puruṣa in the left eye is Indra's wife, the embodiment of his enjoyment (bhogyarupā). The space (ākāśa) inside the fleshy portion of the heart is their tryst. The state of their enjoyment is the consciousness in dream (Taijasa Ātman). The red lump in the heart is their food.

The food when eaten splits into two parts; the gross portion descends downwards while the rest is further cooked by the fire within. It splits again into two portions. The subtle juice becomes blood etcetera and causes growth of the physical body (panch bhoutika pinda-rup śarira). The subtlest portion becomes the red lump of flesh and blood of the subtle body of Indra (linga-deha). Entering into the small veins it nourishes both Indra and his Consort. The innumerable veins and their innumerable holes put together form the cover, as it were, for their bodies when they sleep. The path that they take is the channel which goes upwards from the heart.

The arteries known as hita are established in the heart and issue out from there like a hair divided a thousand fold. Through these hita arteries flows the food. Therefore, the aspect of soul composed by Indra and Virāt (taijasa ātman) is the eater of the better food than the bodily soul (the Vaiśvānara).

In sum, the waking self or the Vaiśvānara ātma alone is the dreaming self or the taijasa ātman. And, then one who moves beyond from that to the deep sleep state or the Prajņā Ātman also realizes that there is the fourth state viz. the Consciousness in Brahma in which all directions; east, west, south, north, upwards and downwards become his vital breath (prāņas). Thus becoming all-pervading Ātman, he too becomes describable only in negative terms namely 'not-this'. He can neither be grasped by the senses or the intellect, nor is He destroyed, contaiminated, attached or pained, nor is He weakened.

"O' Janaka, forsooth, you have now attained the state of fearlessness."

Janaka by now had realized the worthlessness of his offers of cows made to Yājńvalkya, as gifts in return for the instruction imparted. Overwhelmed with the feeling of inadequacy Janaka said, "O Venerable Yājńvalkya, you have imparted the knowledge of fearlessness. I salute you. This country of Videha and my own self are placed at your service. I wish you also to be ever fearless."

* * *

Chapter 18

The Self Alone is Fearless

Dialogue with King Janaka

Prolegomena

As mentioned earlier, the discourses contained in the Third and the Fourth Parts (Brahmaṇas) of the Bṛhadāraṇykopaniṣad describe the Brahma from various stand-points. One may recall that to begin with several reputed scholars of the time engaged Yājṅvalkya in debates covering a variety of issues pertaining to the Vedic rituals and philosophy. Therein Gārgi was told that Brahma was beyond the ambit of mind and logic. Uddālaka was told that Brahma in Its conditioned state was the "thread' that held all beings together and the immortal soul was Inner Controller of all beings. In her second appearance Gārgi was instructed about the Ultimate Reality as the Imperishable One. Eventually, Part Three of the Upaniṣad concludes with describing the Brahma as one, homogeneous, Unlimited, Blissful Consciousness (Chaitanya).

Part Four of the Upanişad opens with the defining and worshipping of Brahma with reference to the divinities that inhabit the various human senses like the speech, vital breath, sight, hearing, mind and heart. The discourse proceeds further to describe the four states in which the ātman dwells, as it were, namely the Vaiśvānara, taijasa, prajņā and turiya. With all this knowledge as his support, King Janaka sheds all fear. Logically, therefore, in the discourse that ensues Brahma is posited as fearlessness (Abhaya).

The Parable

Once, Yājńvalkya went to meet Janaka, the king of Videha. Enroute, he decided to keep his visit a courtesy call and not to initiate a religious dialogue. It so transpired that during an earlier meeting the sage was pleased with the depth of knowledge of the king and had granted him a boon that Janaka could ask a question of his choice whenever he so desired[1]. The king took this opportunity to invoke his privilege and initiated a dialogue on Brahma-Vidyā. He asked questions with regard to the five lights that guide a person.

Janaka: "What light does a person have here (for his guidance)?

Yājńvalkya: 'It is the light of the sun. In that he sits, goes places, and carries on with his activities and returns'.

Janaka: "Yes, it is so. But when the sun has set 'O' Yājńvalkya, what light does a person have here for his guidance?

---

[1] Perhaps this reference to a boon is made only to add an element of drama, a technique usually used in imparting instruction.

Yājńvalkya; "The moon, then is his light. In that light he sits goes places, carries on with his activities and returns."

Janaka: "yes, it is so. But, when the sun has set and the moon has set, O'

Yājńvalkya, what light does a person have here for his guidance?"

Yājńvalkya: "The fire, then, is his light. In that light he sits goes places, carries on with his activities and returns."
Janaka: "Yes, it is so. But when the sun has set and the moon has set and the fire has gone out, O' Yājńvalkya, what light does a person have here for his guidance?"

Yājńvalkya: "The speech, then, is his light. In that light he sits goes places, carries on with his activities and returns. Therefore, O' Emperor, where one does not discern even his own hand, there one goes straight where called."

Janaka: "Yes, it is so. But when the sun has set, and the moon has set, the fire has gone and the speech is hushed, O' Yājńvalkya, what light does a person have here for his guidance?"

Yājńvalkya: "The soul (ātman) alone is his light, then. In that light he sits goes places, carries on with his activities and returns."

Since the soul is self-effulgent and immanent, the question of its not being available for guidance does not arise. Seeing so, Janaka no longer pursues the same line of thought. The answers provided by Yājńvalkya cater for all the three states namely the waking, the dreaming and the deep sleep states of the body-senses aggregate. But the next question seems to show the king's confusion.

Janaka: What is the ātman (Katam ātmayti)?"

[How come that Janaka, an erudite knower of Brahma, should ask such a question? He was perhaps bewildered by the doubt wheather the Ātma Jyoti belonged to the same category as do the lights of the sun, the moon, the eye or the ear that is to say, ether. It could be of external nature like that of the sun and the moon or was of sensory nature as is the case with the light of the eye (fire which include all its manifestations like a lamp and other such appliances) or the ear (space). Alternatively, it could be entirely different from them all. Not being quite sure, he asked the question.]

The doubts that arose in Janaka's mind were not as simple as they are seen prima facie. The answers which the sage Yājńvalkya provided in response, later on generated a host of important issues. In due course of time, thoughts so generated provided sustenance to several philosophical ideologies which were posited as rivals to the Vedānta. Although the vedāntis raised formidable defences against the attacks of their rivals on such issues, the debate countinued unabated. Keeping that story for some other time, we return to Janaka's chambers where Yājńvalkya is all set to propound some of the finest ideas that belong to human heritage.

Yājńvalkya: "He is the vijnānmaya ātman that is the ātman whose light comes in contact with the intellect (buddhi) and which in turn activates the mind along with the senses. That ātman resides in the heart where intellect, too, resides. Yet is this ātman different from all variations of the intellect and the prāṇas (the senses) just as does a tree standing amidst stones. Remaining in consistence with the modifications of the intellect he appears to be thinking and in consistence with the modifications of the senses appears to be conscient. He, when in the dream state, crosses the barriers of all forms of death, namely karma, avidyā and body alongwith all its senses.

"The Being (Ātman, Puruṣa) is said to have born when being invested with body and senses. (The body- senses aggregate is a form of demerit). When about to die this puruṣa leaves the body and senses as also the demerit behind. This transmigration namely passing from life to death corresponds to passing from the waking state into the dream-state. Then, the ātman casts away the body and the senses and revels (sancharati) like light."

"Now, this being has two places, in the main, namely this world and the world-yonder (corresponding respectively to the wakefull consciousness and the deep-sleep states). But there is a third situation viz. an intermediary state corresponding to twilight known as the dream state. While in the intermediary state, He sees both the worlds namely this world and the world yonder. Accordingly, He looks upon pleasures and pains that might be experienced as a result of desires of the previous birth and upon the fruits which might be received during the future one.

"When this being goes to sleep, he takes along all desires of the waking life of this all-providing world, himself dismantles it, himself builds it up and dreams by its own light. In this state this being becomes self-illumined.

"In that state (the state of dream-sleep) there are no chariots, no horses and no roads. But the ātman produces chariots, horses and roads. In that state there are no joys and variety of pleasure but the ātman produces them too. Similarly, though there are no ponds, lakes and rivers but the ātman produces them all. He (the ātman) alone is their creator. The ātman produces them corresponding to the desires of the mind and resultant actions without any assistance or agency like the hands and feet. However, there is no action involved on the part of the ātman. The mind and the sense organs illumined by the light of the conscious self (Chaitanyātma-Jyoti) transform themselves into actions. It therefore seems as if the ātman Itself was the doer.)

During the dream, rendering the body immobile, but being ever-awake and self-illumined the ātman illuminates the sleeping senses. Taking the so illumined senses along, the ātman returns to the waking state. He is the conscious light (chaitanya jyoti) which wanders through the wakefulness and sleep all alone: leaving this dirty nest of the body behind under the care of the vital breath (prāṇa) that Immortal One wanders about freely in pursuit of fulfillment of desires. Assuming forms of various deities and of animals and birds as per His high and low desires. During the dream this Golden Being appears to be enjoying with women, laughing with friends and even getting scared of dreadful animals like tigers.

"The fields of his joyful activities alone become known to all and no one sees that ātman. The doctors say that an asleep should not be woken up suddenly. For, the ātman who has gone out during sleep alongwith the life breath of a particular sense may not return as before. This may cause some irrepairable damage to the particular sense which the ātman had taken along. For this reason, some say that the dream state is a part of the state of wakefulness because one sees during the dream what one sees during wakefulness. But this is not true, for while during wakefulness external lights guide his actions, during the dream state he (the ātman) becomes self-illumined."

Janaka: "O' Venerable One, I present to you a thousand coins for the instruction imparted so far. Pray, instruct me on liberation (mokşa).

Yājńvalkya: "This person having enjoyed the roaming about during the state of deep sleep and having experienced the good and bad fruits (pāpa-puniya) during the sojourn returns to the state of dream by the same route which was taken for going. The ātman, however, remains unconnected with whatever it sees during the state of deep-sleep for, this person (the ātman) is without attachments."

Janaka: "O' Yājńvalkya, quite so. I present to you a thousand coins for imparting this instruction to me. Pray continue with the instruction on the release from the bondage." Yājṅvalkya, "This person having enjoyed during the state of dream-sleep having seen merits and demerits during his sojourn and taking the same path and entrance, returns to the state of wakefulness. Whatever he sees during the state of dream-sleep he remains unconnected with, for, this person is without attachments,"

Janaka: "O' Yājṅvalkya, quite so. I present to you a thousand coins for imparting this instruction to me. Pray instruct me further about the release from bondage."

Yājṅvalkya: "This person having enjoyed during the state of wakefulness, having seen merits and demerits during his sojourn and taking the same path and entrance returns to the state of dream.

"As a large big fish moves from one bank to the other bank of a river alternating, even so does this person move alternating between these two conditions, viz. the condition of dreem-sleep and the condition of wakefulness.

"Just as a hawk or an eagle soars high in the sky but on being exhausted by its intensive flights returns to the nest for taking rest, so does this ātman after incessant wanderings through the two states of dream-sleep and wakefulness becomes tired and hastens to the place of rest where in sleep this person entertains no desires nor does he have any dreams."

[In his commentary Śankrāchārya at places provides a fleeting reference of the released soul while referring to the deep-sleep state. This must not be understood as if the two states are the same or similar. The released soul forsakes for ever all connections with all the states of the gross body, subtle body and the causal body. But the deep-sleep is a state which by itself is an attachment. Therefore, there is no similarity between the two.]

There are spread throughout the body of person innumerable veins (hita-nādi) which are as thin as a hairsplit in thousand parts. In these veins is filled the sap of different hues namely white, blue, yellow, green and red. In this network of veins, reside the subtle body (the linga śarir) comprising seventeen constituents – five basic elements, ten organs of senses and action, prāṇa and the antahkaraṇa (the mind, the intellect, the attention and the ego complex). This subtle body is the shelter and support of desires and in that the man dreams about women, chariots, elephants and the like. In this state, because of the desires prompted by the spell of ignorance (avidyā-janit vāsnā) the dreamer feels being killed, as it were, or being chased by an elephant, as it were or falling into a ditch, as it were. Thus, whatever this person experiences during the state of wakefulness the same he believes to be seeing during dream. All this is because of ignorance. When believing that he is a god or a king he thinks 'I am all this', that is his highest world (param-loka).

[The sage then proceeds to elaborate upon the state of deep sleep].

"That is the Ātman without a desire, free from good and evil and harbouring no fear".

[The concept is made clear by Yājńvalkya with the help of an entirely mundane example.]

"As a man, when in the sexual embrace of his beloved wife knows nothing of within or of without, so this Ātman when in the embrace of the pure consciousness (prajńātmā) knows nothing of within or of without. [The meaning is that all notions of duality are resolved.] That is the state of total fulfillment of desires (āpta-kāma), of residing in its own desire (ātma-kāma), of being without desire (akām) and of having shed all sorrows (śoka-śunya).

[All worldly relations like that of father and son or mother and progeny have reference to a particular action (karma). All other aspects like piety and knowledge ability and even crimes, too, are connected with corresponding actions. In sum, all aspects connected with life are tied up with actions which in turn are tied up with desires. Since during sleep one reaches the state of desirelessness, there remains no likelihood of karma and consequently all attachments are forsaken.]

"During the deep-sleep stage a father remains not a father, a mother remains not a mother, worlds no longer remain worlds, gods remain no more gods and vedas remain no more Vedas. Here (in this state) the thief is no more a thief, a killer of a Brāhmin is no more so and a chāndāla (son of a śudra from a Brāhmin wife) is no more a chāndāla or a paulkasa (son of a śudra from a Kṣatriya mother) no more a paulkasa, a mendicant no more a mendicant and an ascetic is no longer an ascetic. During this state this being (puruṣa) is neither attached to merits (punya) nor to evils (pāpam). He goes across all sorrows of his heart".

(Since sorrows are the outcomes of unfulfilled desires, there can be no sorrow where there is no desire, as is the case during the state of deep-sleep).

The clarification may be sought at this stage, if ātman is ever-consciousness how come it does not see during the state of deep-sleep. The answer is provided thus: "He (the ātman) who does not see (with the eyes), sees not (the objects of usual seeing) while seeing as there is no cessation of sight of the seer, who is imperishable. There then is no second other than and separate from this seer that he may see".

(The logic of this thought needs to be understood in the right perspective. The ordinary process of seeing comprises four constituents namely the seer, the instrument of seeing (the eye) the object of seeing and the light manifesting the object. If any of these constituents is missing the process of physical seeing will not take place. But the ātman is not an ordinary seer. It neither needs an instrument to see, nor an external light for manifestation of objects (being self illumined) and above all, there is nothing other than it which may be seen. So the process of seeing by the ātman, as it were, is not comparable with the seeing done under the spell of avidyā by the body-senses aggregate. The same logic applies to other sense experiences stated here after).

"He, who does not smell, smells not (the objects of usual smelling) while smelling as there is no cessation of smell of the smeller who is imperishable. There then is no second other than and separate from this smeller that he may smell.

"He, who does not taste, tastes not (the objects of usual tasting) while tasting as there is no cessation of taste of the taster, who is imperishable. There then is no second other than and separate from the taster that he may taste.

"He who does not speak, speaks not (the objects of usual speech) while speaking, as there is no cessation of speech of this speaker, who is imperishable. There then is no second other than and separate from this speaker that he may speak about.

"He who does not hear, hears not (the objects of usual hearing) while hearing as there is no cessation of hearing of this hearer, who is imperishable. There then is no second, other than and separate from this hearer that he may hear about.

"He who does not think, thinks not (the objects of usual thinking) while thinking as there is no cessation of thinking of this thinker, who is imperishable. There then is no second other than and separate from this thinker that he may think about.

"He who does not touch, touches not (the objects of usual touch) while touching as there is no cessation of touch of the toucher, who is imperishable. There then is no second, other than and separate from this toucher that he may touch.

"He, who does not know, knows not (the objects of usual knowledge) while knowing as there is no cessation of knowing of the knower, who is imperishable. There then is no second other than and separate from this knower that he may know particularly about.

Where (during the wakeful and the dream-sleep states) there seems to be another born of ignorance (avidyā-janit) there the one might see the other; the one might smell the other; the one might taste the other; the one might address the other; the one might taste the other; the one might think about the other; the one might touch the other; the one might know the other.

"As the reflection in the water is the evidence of the purity of the water itself (transparency is the evidence) so is the deep-sleep witness of this seer, the One without a second"

So was Janaka instructed by Yājńvalkya, "O' Emperor, this is the world of Brahma (Brahma loka: Where Brahma is the world), this is his (puruṣa's) final destiny (param-gati), this is his ultimate treasure (param-sampatti), and this is his ultimate abode (param loka), and this is his highest bliss (param-ānand). It is on a fraction of this bliss, all other beings [those who pursue sensuous pleasures] live."

[Blessings come in three forms; pleasure (sukha), joy (harṣa) and bliss (ānanda). Pleasure is the satisfying of our physical senses of tasting, hearing, touching, seeing and smelling. The pleasure stays only so long as the concerned sense is in direct connect with the object providing satisfaction and no more. The senses possess no ability to cross the barrier of time and space. The joy denotes the extension of a satisfying experience beyond the bounds of time and space through the 'inward eye' viz. the mind (manas). Its quality and longevity depend on the conditioning of the mind of experiencer. The mind possesses, though limited, the quality to cross the barrier of time and space. It also has the unique power to look into itself, discriminate and modify an experience. The bliss is eternal fulfillment or the ultimate satisfaction unrelated to the manifest world. This is believed to belong to the seamless domain of Ātman, as it were.]

Then, the sage explained as to whatever he meant by the phrase, 'a fraction of this bliss' (that of Paramānanda).

"The pleasures of the one who is of sound body, whose all limbs and sense organs are perfectly efficient, who is fortunate to possess all material resources that provide earthly pleasure, who is the lord and master of men like him and who is best provided for, in the material sense, represents one unit of pleasure and that is the ultimate of human pleasure (manuṣyāṇām-ānanda).

"A hundred-fold bliss of humans is one unit of bliss of those who have won the worlds of the fathers (pitṛloka).

"A hundred-fold bliss of the world of fathers is one unit of bliss of those who have won the world of the Gandharvas.

"A hundred-fold bliss of the world of Gandharvas is one unit of bliss of the world of those who attain god-hood because of their meritorious deeds (Karma-devas).

"A hundred fold bliss of the karam-devas is one unit of bliss of the world of born-gods (ājān-devas) and of those who have learnt the Vedas, are sinless and have shed all desires.

"A hundred-fold the bliss of born-gods and of those who have learnt the Vedas, are sinless and have shed all desires is one unit of bliss of the world of Prajāpati (Prajāpati loka).

"A hundred-fold the bliss of the world of Prajāpati and of those who have learnt the Vedas, are sinless and have shed all desires is one unit of bliss of the world of Brahma (Brahmaloka). And, this is the highest bliss (Pramānanda).

O' Emperor, this is (the state of Brahma) Brahamaloka," So said Yājńvalkya.

Janaka: "I offer a thousand cows to you, O' Venerable one. Pray, continue to impart instruction to me regarding liberation from the bondage of life and death."

At this stage, there arose a sense of apprehension in the mind of Yājńvalkya who thought to himself, 'this shrewd and intelligent king has tied me down from all aspects. Having known the answer to a question, he proceeds to raise another one. This way, he wants to acquire my entire knowledge on the subject'. All the same, he continues with the discourse.

"And this person (puruṣa) having enjoyed and wandered about during the dream state and thus having gone through the good and the evil experiences (punyas) and pāpas) hastens back to the state of wakefulness by the same route which he had taken to go out."

Then, Yājńvalkya proceeded to describe the moment of death. "Just as a rickety cart moves with a rattle when heavily loaded (with house-hold goods) even so the soul which has acquired a body (śarir-ātman) makes a rattling noise (when breathing becomes difficult at the approach of death) under the burden of the subtle body (the linga deha). While leaving this body, it appears to be going through a great measure of pain, as if all the vitals were being torn asunder[2]."

How and why does all this happen? The answer is given thus: "When the body becomes too weak due to old age or

---

[2] As the divinities inhabiting the sense organs; for instance, the āditya of the eye and vāyu of the nose return to their respective sources such as the sun and the air, the sense organs stop functioning.

illness then just as the ripe fruit of mango or of a fig or a peepal tree gets detached from the tree and falls down, so does this person (jiva) get detached from his limbs. Then, taking the path by which it had entered this body, it moves on to another which is made ready for him in accordance with his past actions and the state of knowledge.

The situation of the prāṇa leaving this body (urdhvochhasa) is witnessed by human beings everyday. The śruti describes it there out of sympathy so as to create among the people a desire for detachment. Since at the moment of death one is not in a position to perform a meritorious act, the teaching is that good acts should be done well before that stage actually arrives.

"As lords of the realm, magistrates, chariot drivers and village-headmen wait for the arrival of their king with presents of food, drink and a done-up lodging and on his reaching there say, 'Here comes he!, Here comes he! So do all these elements (bhutas) wait for this person at the time of birth. Keeping all things ready for him (so that he enjoys the fruits of his karmas) they (the bhutas) welcome him saying, 'Here comes the Brahma! Here comes He!'

"And when they (the bhutas) come to know that he is coming, they gather together and come forward out of volition to welcome him."

"As the lords of the realm, magistrates, chariot drivers and village headmen gather around their king at the time of his departure even so do all the breaths gather round the departing soul and leave with him as he breathes his last.

"When this ātman becomes weak, as it were or unconscious, as it were then all the breaths (of the senses like the organ of speech etcetera) gather around it. Then he (the Jiva) collects up all these energy-factors (tejo-mātrā) and retires to its self illumined source ie the ātman to dwell in the space within the heart.

'At that stage though he has eyes but he cannot see, becoming unconscious he loses the ability to recognize forms.

"When the sense of sight merges with the subtle-body, (lingātmā) people say he (the person) sees no more.'

"When the sense of smell merges with the subtle-body, the people say he smells no more'.

"When the sense of speech merges with the subtle body, the people say 'he speaks no more.'

"When the sense of hearing merges with the subtle body the people says 'he hears no more.'

"When the mind merges with the subtle body, the people say 'he thinks no more'.

"When the sense of touch merges with the subtle body, the people say 'he feels (the touch) no more.'

"When the intelligence merges with the subtle body, the people say 'he knows no more.'

"Then, the outward path[3] (the upper end) of the heart becomes illumined. Taking that light, the ātman leaves for its destination either through the eye (if the world of light ie. the āditya-lok, is to be attained) or through the head (if it were to reach the Brahma-lok) or through some other outlet of the body.

[The outward route is dependent on the nature of the accumulated deeds and the quality of knowledge of the embodied soul.]

"The vital breath (prāṇa) follows the ātman and all other breaths (those identified with various senses) follow the vital breath. At this stage he gains a particular consciousness (Viśeṣa Vijnānvān) but not by his own volition. This consciousness is conditioned by his knowledge (vidyā),

---

3 The outward route is dependent on the nature of the accumulated deeds and the quality of knowledge of the embodied soul

works (karmani) and previous intelligence (purva-prajńā). He then in their company departs for the regions as willed.

"Just as a caterpillar having reached the farthest end of the blade of grass gathers together closely all its parts till such time that it takes hold of another blade even so the desire (vāsanā) guided by avidyā and karma when stuck up in the heart in the body which the ātman is about to leave as it were, begins to create a subtle body and plans to leave the old one only when the Jiva is sufficiently attached to the new one. Then this vāsnā putting the earlier body to the state of unconsciousness takes the support of the other and acquires attachment in it.

"Just as a goldsmith moulds a piece of the available gold into a variety of beautiful forms even so the ātman moulds such newer and more beautiful bodies out of the existing elements of māyā which are worthy of occupancy by the Fathers, the Gandharvas, the Devas and the Prajāpati or other beings.

"Forsooth, that ātman is Brahma, made of knowledge (vijńāna mayaħ), of mind (mano mayaħ), of life (prāno mayaħ), of sight (chakşur mayaħ), of hearing (śrotra mayāh), of earth (pṛthvi mayaħ), of water (āpo mayaħ), of air (vāyu-mayaħ), of space (ākāśo mayaħ), of energy (tejo mayaħ), of non-energy (atejo mayaħ), of desire (kāma mayaħ), of non-desire (akāma mayaħ), of anger (Krodha mayaħ), of non-anger (akrodha mayaħ), of virtuousness (dharma mayaħ), of non-virtuousness (adharma mayaħ) and of the self (Svam mayaħ). It is made of everything.

Verily, therefore, the Ātman is said to be 'made of this'[4] and is 'made of that'[5]. It becomes in accordance with

---

[4] That which is perceived.

[5] That which is inferred.

the jivātmā's actions and conduct. The one who performs good actions becomes good while the one who performs evil actions becomes evil. The one who performs works of merit (punya karmas) becomes meritorious and the one who performs works of demerit (pāpa-karmas) becomes bad (pāpi). Some people say that a person is made of desires only (Kama mayah̃). As is one's desire, so does one resolve; as is one's resolution, so does one act and as are one's actions so are the fruits for him."

The desires dictate the destiny and the nature of mokṣa of a desireless knower of Brahma.

"There is a verse in this regard: 'Where one's mind is intensely attached one transmigrates thereto together with the actions for enjoying their fruits. Whatever one does in this world one enjoys their fruits in that world (the world after-death) and then returns to this world of action again. Only he, who desires is so destined."

What is the position of the one who entertains no desires, who is without desire, who is free from desires, whose desires have been satisfied and whose object of desire is the self itself?

"In his case the prāṇas do not desert him. Being the Brahma, he goes to Brahma.

[Since a knower of Brahma sees nothing other than and separate from the Ātman, there remains nothing other than and separate from the Ātman for him to desire. So, there remains no desire and that stage is the termination of ignorance. Thereafter, even if the self remains embodied and carries on its routine, it is no longer attached to the karmas and their results. Thus is the liberation from the bondage of life and death obtained.]

"When all the desires that take shelter in one's heart are totally shed, this mortal becomes Immortal and becomes the Brahma even when still residing in the body. There is a parable in this regard. Just as the slough cast off by a snake keeps lying dead on the anthill, even so this body remains of no consequence. Verily, the prāṇa, which is without body (aśriri) is Brahma; the Light."

Janaka: "O' Respectable Sir, I present a thousand cows to you."

[The knower of Brahma whose desire is the Ātman alone is released from the bondage of life and death. And what happens to those whose actions are motivated by desires and to those who remain unaffected by desires?]

Yājńvalkya: "There are verses regarding this. This path of knowledge (Jńāna-mārga) verily is subtle, vast and ancient. I have come in contact with it and have been completely satisfied by treading upon it. The courageous people who are knowers of Brahma by following this path achieve liberation even when alive. And, after leaving this body they go to the worlds of light (achieve realization) by the same path.

"Those who follow the path of knowledge as a means to obtain liberation describe it in different ways some say it is white (śukla and śudha), others say it is blue, yellow, green or red. But this path is laid by Brahma Itself (by those souls which have travelled on it and by giving up all desires have known the Ultimate Reality.) By this path, the one who has known the Brahma and thereby has become meritorious and lustrous (punyakṛt and taijasa) alone goes.

"They who worship non-knowledge (avidyā or karma) being ignorant enter darkness and those who remain involved in the delight of vidyā go into yet deeper darkness as it were[6].

---

6 That is to say, those who follow only the ritual part of the Vedas without taking due cognizance of the knowledge contained in the Upaniṣads.

"Those people who are bereft of knowledge of self go after death to those worlds which are joyless and filled with darkness.

"If a person realizes his soul and comes to think 'I am He.' He shall be left with nothing to desire for. And, for what end to serve would he cling to this body! "That knower of truth, who has found and realized the ātman that has entered the body – which, as if, is an amalgam of complexities and calamities – is the maker of everything (viśvakṛtā) for he is the creator of all[7]. Each soul (loka) is his and he is the soul itself.

"Should we be able to realize the self so, in the self-mode (ātam-bhāva) while still dwelling in this body, we must consider ourselves fortunate. Otherwise, we suffer a great deal of damage and remain ignorant. Those who come to know Him so, become immortals, while others suffer miseries and sorrows as victims of the continued cycle of births and deaths. [Unfortunately, the latter category of people considers the body as self.] "A person, who following the instruction received from a kind teacher, directly realizes the self which is self-illumined, is the bestower of fruits of one's actions and is the lord of the past, present and future, he does not stay away from Him. Nor does he talk ill of others.

"On that Immortal Light (the light of all lights, under whose command the time moves on as days and nights, gods meditate as 'the Ageless'. [Since they meditate on the attribute of agelessness of that light they live long lives.] "That in Him rests the five-folds[8]. I regard that soul as

---

7 The expression 'loka' here means the soul, meaning thereby that all the souls are his and he is the soul of all. Śankarāchārya.

8 Either the five; Gandhrvas, pitṛs, devas, asuras, (demons) and rākṣasa (monsters); or the five viz. the four castes and the untouchables or the five prāṇas and the space.

the Immortal Brahma. I, the knower of that Brahma am Immortal[9].

"They who come to know him as the vital breath of the vital breath, the eye of the eye, the ear of the ear and the mind of the mind have realized that ancient primeval Brahma.

"The Brahma is to be seen from the eye of the mind alone. [Following of course, the instruction imparted by a competent preceptor]. There is in It no diversity. He, who sees diversity in It, as it were, gets death after death.

"The Brahma should be realized as a unity, the unknowable, ever constant, spotless, subtler than the space, unborn soul, infinite and immortal.

"For knowing him, an intelligent seeker of truth should make efforts to acquire pure intellect[10] (prajńā) which alone resolves all conflicts. One need not meditate upon many a word[11] for that merely is exercising the organ of speech to weariness.

"That great Unborn Self, permeating the intellect (Vijńāna mayāh) is identified with breaths (prāṇas of the sense organs) dwells in the space inside the heart. It is the controller of all, the ruler of all (one who rules without a hierarchy, as it were) and is the lord of all. Neither is its greatness enhanced through good deeds nor is it reduced through evil ones. It is supreme lord, ruler and protector

---

9 Since Yājńvalkya had shed all ignorance, he could describe himself as immortal.

10 These efforts include reclusion (sanyās), control of ego (Sama), control of senses (dama), renunciation (uparati), tolerance (titikṣā) and contemplation (smādhikā).

11 This position is to be taken to refute the idea of diversity and to propound the idea of unity.

of all beings. It is the bridge between various worlds maintaining their separate identities and boundaries. (The reference here is to the various worlds (loka) where living beings go to reap the fruits of their actions. These worlds are located apart by the divine law so as to avoid confusion).

The seekers of truth realize this Self through the study of the Vedas, through performing sacrifices, through giving of alms and gifts and through practicing such austerities which are attached to no desires. Knowing it alone one becomes a religious thinker (a muni)[12]. In pursuit of this world of self alone, the mendicants (tyāgi-puruṣas) renounce their homes (that is, the house-holders' life of rituals seeking worldly rewards).

The wisemen of yore renounced all desires concerning offsprings because they thought that once this self had been realized this world has been attained, no purpose was served by begetting offsprings. They, therefore, gave up all desires for sons (putreṣṇā), for wealth (vitteṣṇā) and for the world (lokeṣṇā) and led the life of mendicants (bhikṣāchārya). That which is the desire for sons indeed is the desire for wealth and that which is the desire for wealth indeed is the desire for world; for both these are desires.

That Ātman has been described as 'Not this, not this' (meaning thereby that It is neither connected with the means nor with the end and is free from all relative attributes.) It is unseizable because it connot be seized; It is undecaying because it never decays; It is unattached because It is never attached; It is unfettered because It is beyond the pale of pain or injury.

---

[12] Mananānmuniḥ, the one who meditates deeply on religious issues.

"The knower of Brahma is not affected by his deeds, good or bad; that is to say, he crosses that threshold of feeling guilty for doing what was undesirable or the feeling of elation for doing what was desirable. He is neither afflicted by what he does or by what he does not do. (The deeds and actions refer to performance of prescribed rites, rituals and sacrifices which result into certain fruits to be reaped).

[This does not mean that they are absolved of all worldly consequences of their actions.]

"This has been said in a verse of the Ṛgveda: This is the eternal glory of the knower of Brahma. This glory is said to be eternal and thereby changeless because it is neither enhanced through good deeds nor is it reduced through evil ones[13].

"One should therefore know That One alone. Knowing that, one is not affected by evil actions.

"Therefore, he who knows 'That' as such becomes calm, subdued, withdrawn, tolerant and collected; he sees the Self within the self (body). He sees all as the Self. He is not affected by evil and goes beyond the reach of the evil. The evil does not afflict him, he, in turn, demolishes all evil. Verily, he becomes sinless and desireless knower of Brahma.

"O' Emperor, this is the world of Brahma and you have reached that (with the help of Yājńvalkya)" so said Yājńvalkya.

---

13 As per Vedānta philosophy both the righteous and the unrighteous actions belong to the phenomenal world which is impermanent. The glory of the Brahma, so to say, is permanent and therefore unaffected by the deeds whatever.

Janaka: "O' Venerable Sir, I present to you the entire Videh country and surrender myself, too, to wait upon you."

[Here ends the dialogue]

Summing up the instruction, the sage said: "That great Unborn Self is undecaying, immortal, undying, fearless and infinite. Brahma alone is fearless. [Because It alone is beyond the pale of death, decay or injury.] He who knows it thus becomes the Fearless Brahma."

This verse contains the gist of the philosophy permeating the dialogue: the non-duality and immortality of the infinitesimal ātman and its complete identity with the Infinite Brahma. In order to make the teaching comprehensible, non-duality has been explained through such means as mention of creation and preservation etc. but to eliminate the impression of duality the Ultimate Reality has been described as "Not this, not this", at times even as 'Not This' (that what is perceived), Not that' (that what is inferred).

Chapter 19

All is the Self Alone

Dialogue with Maitreyi

Prolegomena

This parable is contained in Chapter Four of Part Two and in Chapter Five of Part four of the *Bṛhadāraṇykopaniṣad.* Muni Yājṅvalkya had two wives namely, Katyāni and Maitreyi. While Katyāni was good as a traditional housewife, Maitreyi, the younger of the two shared the philosophical interests of her renowned husband. Indeed, her own accomplishments in the field of Vedic lore were well known.

The theme of this dialogue is the Non-duality of Brahma; the sumum bonum of the Upaniṣadic teaching. Having lived a full life as a householder Yājṅvalkya decided to embrace the life of an ascetic (sanyāsin). The Vedic code prescribes that a man can renounce the world during the life-time of his wife only with her expressed consent. Yājṅvalkya, therefore, approached his younger wife with this proposal.

The Parable

Yājńvalkya "O' Maitreyi, I desire to renounce the world and embrace the life of a recluse. For that purpose, O' dear, I seek your concurrence before making the necessary settlement between you and Katyāni.'

Maitreyi: "O' Venerable Sir, should this whole world filled with all riches be given to me, would I become immortal thereby?"

Yājńvalkya: "No. Your life will be just like that of those people who possess plenty. There is no hope of becoming immortal through wealth."

Maitreyi: 'What shall I do with that which would not make me immortal? Kindly spare only that (part of your possessions) for me which will lead me to immortality."

The sage felt happy on hearing the request of his wife and spoke;

Yājńvalkya: "You have always been dear to me and now you say what pleases me the most. Come hither, I shall tell you all about that (which will lead you to immortality.) Do apply your mind deeply to what I say."

Yājńvalkya commenced his discourse with describing the *raison d'etre* of non-attachment as an essential factor of renunciation. His instruction on non-attachment establishes the premise that all human relations and other objects that promise enjoyment always come closer to our hearts. It is not easy to forsake such attractions unless their real worth becomes known[1]. He, therefore, declaimed:

---

[1] That is to say, that once one becomes aware that such relationships and objects indeed are not the source of real enjoyment, all attraction for them wears off.

"Verily, not for the sake of the husband, my dear, is the husband loved, but the husband is loved for the sake of the self (the ātman)[2].

"Verily, not for the sake of the wife, my dear, is the wife loved, but the wife is loved for the sake of the self.

"Verily, not for the sake of the progeny, my dear, are the progeny loved, but the progeny are loved for the sake of the self.

"Verily, not for the sake of the riches, my dear, are the riches loved, but the riches are loved for the sake of the self.

"Verily, not for the sake of Brāhmaṇahood is a Brāhmaṇa dear, a Brāhmaṇ is dear for the sake of the self.

"Verily, not for the sake of Kṣātrahood is a Kṣatriya dear, a Kṣatriya is dear for the sake of the self.

"Verily, not for the sake of the worlds are worlds dear, the worlds are dear for the sake of the self.

"Verily not for the sake of the gods are the gods dear, the gods are dear for the sake of the self.

"Verily, not for the sake of the beings are the beings dear, the beings are dear for the sake of the self.

"Verily, not for the sake of all (meaning the rest) are all dear, all are dear for the sake of the Self.

"O' Maitreyi, it is the Self (Ātman) alone that is worth realizing, worth hearing and worth reflecting and

---

2 The teaching herein is that objects void of self (soul) can offer no pleasure to the Self (the Ultimate Being). Nor can an object which is void of self offer any attraction to a similar object because no dead matter can be dear to the dead matter. The real attraction is because of the indwelling self (the individual ātman) which indeed is the Supreme Soul, only appearing as such due to ignorance (māyā or avidyā).

meditating upon. On realizing the Self, through reflection and meditation O' dear, all this becomes known[3].

"The Brāhmaņ rejects the one who sees him different from the Self. The Kşatriya rejects the one who sees him different from the Self. The worlds reject the one who sees them different from the Self. The gods reject the one who sees them different from the Self. The beings reject the one who sees them different from the Self. [Why is it so?] All these Brāhmaņs, Kşatriyas, worlds, gods, beings and the rest are nothing but the Self alone."

[Question: How could it be said that everything was Self?]

Answer: It is so because consciousness (Chitta), which is an aspect of Self essentially, abides in everything. This is explained through some illustrations.

"As the various specific notes of a drum, when it is beaten, can not be grasped per se, but are grasped only when the general sound produced (cumulatively) by the specific strokes is grasped[4].

"As the various specific notes of a conch shell, when it is blown, can not be grasped per se, but are, grasped only when the general sound produced by the blowing of the specific strokes is grasped.

"As the various specific notes of a viņā (Indian harp) when it is played upon, can not be grasped per se, but are grasped only when the general sound produced by playing on the strings with specific strokes is grasped[5].

---

3 It is so because Self alone is everything. There is nothing other than the Self. This thought is explained through the next verse.

4 That is to say, the constituent notes can not be grasped apart from the whole sound of a beat. They all therefore are the sound alone.

5 By the same logic, no separate objects can be perceived in the waking or the dream states, apart from consciousness. Just as

Yājńvalkya then told Maitreyi as to how the Brahma (ātma) was the source of all knowledge. "O, Maitreyi! As various kinds of smokes issue forth from the fire kindled with the wet fuel, so have issued forth like the breath of the Infinite Being these Rg Veda, Yajur Veda, Sāma Veda, Atharvaṇāgiras (Atharva Veda), history (itihāsa), mythology (purāṇa), education (vidyā), the Upaniṣads, verses (slokas), aphorisms (sutras), expositions (anuvyākhyānas) and commentaries (vyākhyānas). From It, indeed, are all these breathed forth."

The Brahma is not only the source and sustenance of all but also is the ultimate goal or end of all. This point is elucidated thus : "As the ocean is the ultimate tryst [where they meet] of all water-bodies so is the skin the ultimate tryst of all kinds of touches, nostrils are the ultimate tryst of all kinds of smells, tongue is the ultimate tryst of all kinds of tastes, eyes are the ultimate tryst of all kinds of forms, ears are the ultimate tryst of all kinds of sounds, mind is the ultimate tryst of all forms of resolutions, heart is the ultimate tryst of all knowledge, hands are the one goal of all activity, the organ of generation is the one goal of all pleasures, the organ of excretions is the one goal of all excretions, the feet are the one goal of all paths similarly, the speech (vāk) is the one goal or the ultimate tryst of all the Vedas."

The general functions of all the sensory and motor organs merge into the vital breath (prāṇa) like all the water bodies merge into the ocean. And, indeed the Vital Breath (prāṇa) is identical with the pure Intelligence ie prajṇā.

---

are the various specific notes included in the general tone even so are all diverse entities unified in Brahma or Consciousness.

The universe comprising names and forms has no existence apart from the Brahma at any state; that is to say at the time of its beginning or during its continuance or its dissolution like the bubbles or the foam can have no existence apart from its cause viz. water at any point of time. Therefore, Brahma is to be realized as one Pure Intelligence. The sage further explained the process of dissolution. In the cosmic context dissolution signifies cessation of the phenomenal existence or Pralaya. In the context of the embodied soul it means the cessation of ignorance leading to knowledge of the Ultimate Reality. Such a knower becomes integral to the Pure Intelligence where there remains no possibility of Ignorance (Avidyā) casting its spell on him for a return to the phenomenal world. This thought is illustrated thus:

"As a lump of salt when dropped into the water (the ocean where the salt comes from) dissolves into it and it remains no longer possible to take the lump out even though the entire water bears its taste (proving its existence). O' dear Maitreyi, even so this Great Being (Mahad-bhuta) endless and infinite is the mass of Pure Intelligence (Vijṅānaghana). Arising out of the elements (as a separate entity) this self (ātman) vanishes alongwith them. Once the body is shed, there remains no more consciousness. So say I." So said Yājṅvalkya.

The statement 'once the body is shed, there remains no more consciousness' bewildered[6] Maitreyi and she asked her husband to explain the point.

Yājṅvalkya: "O' Maitreyi, verily I have stated nothing which should bewilder you. This is sufficient for

---

6 That the Self which in reality is homogeneous consciousness, on shedding the body it loses this quality had bewildered Maitreyi.

understanding the Reality. I now tell you as to how there remain no more of particular consciousness after death. Listen.

"For where there is duality, as it were, there one smells the other, there one sees the other, there one tastes the other, there one hears the other, there one speaks to another, there one thinks of another there one touches the other, there one understands another. But, where everything has become the self, who should smell whom and through what, who should see whom and through what, who should taste whom and through what, who should hear whom and through what, who should speak to whom and through what, who should think of whom and through what, who should touch whom and through what and who should understand whom and through what? Through what should one know That through which all this is known? This Self is that which has been described as 'Not this, not this.' That is not comprehensible for It never comprehends; That is un-decaying for It never decays; That is un-attached for It is never attached; That is unfettered for It never feels pain or suffers injury.

"Through what medium O' Maitreyi could one know the knower?"[7].

"You have been imparted instruction in this way. Verily, O' Maitreyi, this knowledge alone is the means of attaining Immortality.

Having said all this Yājńvalkya become a sanyāsin.

---

[7] On realization of the Non-dual Self, there can remain no consciousness of actions, their factors or results.

Index